THE ELITE FORCES
HANDBOOK OF
UNARMED
COMBAT

THE ELITE FORCES HANDBOOK OF
UNARMED COMBAT

Ron Shillingford

THOMAS DUNNE BOOKS

ST. MARTIN'S GRIFFIN
NEW YORK

Copyright ©Amber Books Ltd 2000

Reprinted in 2008

THOMAS DUNNE BOOKS
An imprint of St. Martin's Press.
All rights reserved.
No part of this book may be used or reproduced in any manner whatsoever without written permission except in the case of brief quotations embodied in critical articles or reviews. For information, address St. Martin's Press, 175 Fifth Avenue, New York, N.Y. 10010.

ISBN 0-312-26436-4
EAN 978-0-312-26436-9

Editorial and design by:
Amber Books Ltd
Bradley's Close,
74-77 White Lion Street
London N1 9PF
www.amberbooks.co.uk

Editor: Helen Wilson
Design: Hawes Design
Picture research: Lisa Wren
Artworks: Chris West, Black Hat Ltd

This book is for informational purposes only. It is not intended for use as a training manual of any kind. Readers should not use any of the unarmed combat or other military techniques described in this book for any purpose whatsoever.

Printed in Thailand

10 9 8 7 6 5 4

Contents

CHAPTER 1   **ESSENTIALS OF UNARMED COMBAT**   **6**

CHAPTER 2   **THE MARTIAL ARTS HERITAGE**   **22**

CHAPTER 3   **TRAINING KEPT SIMPLE**   **40**

CHAPTER 4   **MENTAL TRAINING**   **62**

CHAPTER 5   **VULNERABLE AREAS OF THE BODY**   **72**

CHAPTER 6   **PUNCHING AND KICKING**   **84**

CHAPTER 7   **BLOCKS AGAINST PUNCHES AND KICKS**   **96**

CHAPTER 8   **CHOKES AND HEADLOCKS**   **102**

CHAPTER 9   **BREAKING FREE**   **120**

CHAPTER 10   **THROWS**   **134**

CHAPTER 11   **GOING TO GROUND**   **142**

CHAPTER 12   **DEFENCE AGAINST A FIREARM**   **150**

CHAPTER 13   **DEFENCE AGAINST KNIFE ATTACK**   **160**

CHAPTER 14   **DEFENCE AGAINST BAYONET ATTACK**   **174**

CHAPTER 15   **DEFENCE AGAINST CLUBS AND TRUNCHEONS**   **180**

CHAPTER 16   **MULTIPLE ASSAILANTS**   **184**

INDEX   **190**

Essentials of Unarmed Combat

Military unarmed combat is integral to the development of the pure martial arts, and substantially pre-dates the more organised later practices. Babylonian artwork from 2000 BC, for instance, shows soldiers practising what appears to be block-and-counter manoeuvres and wrestling.

A ncient Mesopotamian martial practices probably developed with trade contact with northern Indian cultures, which also have a long history of unarmed combat, and indeed it is to the East that we must look for some of the earliest developments in modern military unarmed combat. Before China established itself as a nation in 500 BC, its territory was home to a multitude of frequently warring feudal states. The conflict ranged from set-piece battles between armies to one-on-one fights before royal audiences, and unarmed combat became a necessary practice for soldiers who wanted both to survive in action and gain esteem in the eyes of the court. Yet from the 6th century BC and particularly from when China became an integrated nation, professional unarmed combat

LEFT: Soldiers from the Spetsnaz, the Soviet special forces, working with the frontier force during the conflict in Afghanistan, take time out from operations to indulge in some karate. Spetsnaz unarmed combat stresses lethal strikes.

skills were especially in demand along dangerous trade routes throughout the Chinese hinterland and across to India and the Middle East. Bandits and assassins were prevalent along these routes, and military and ex-military personnel found themselves guarding merchants, VIPs and trade caravans. Their skills were frequently called upon, and their lives as bodyguards could be brutal and short.

Meanwhile, India had charted a similar development in terms of military unarmed combat skills. Inter-Indian state rivalries in the second half of the first millennium BC had made unarmed combat skills a necessity. Yet for the warrior classes (mainly from aristocratic families) martial skills were the signature of one accomplished in culture and war, as laid down by the advice of the mythical figure of Agastiya. Ancient Indian temples often feature carvings of gods and men locked in unarmed combat using many of the blocks and strikes seen today.

Once trade routes between China and India expanded, ideas of unarmed combat were exchanged between the armies of the East and these ideas would form the basis of unarmed combat development in the first millennium AD. Yet the West had also developed its own traditions of military martial art, though somewhat later than Eastern ideas. The gladiatorial traditions of the classical Greek and Roman cultures doubtless infused the ancient Mediterranean armies and occupied lands with many

unarmed skills, yet the Western focus tended to remain on skills in handling weaponry. However, the much later medieval period evidences a large range of military texts which amply illustrated grappling, wrestling, blocking techniques, throws and disarming techniques (usually as ancillary skills to the instruction of swordsmanship). Texts such as Fiore de Liberi's *Flos Duellatorum* of 1410 and Charles Studer's *Das Solothurner Fechtbuch* of 1423 both contained sections on unarmed grappling techniques in addition to the sections on weapons like the longsword and the dagger. Yet it was the development in weapon technology which would steadily constrict the practice of

LEFT: **Soldiers from the Swiss Army practise various holds at the Isone Grenadier School. Groundwork is an essential part of a soldier's training. There are two categories: fighting from the floor and grappling on the floor.**

BELOW: **Egyptian special forces practise. The soldiers on the right have thrown their opponents to the ground and are about to finish them off with a hard kick. Good footwork and balance is essential in unarmed combat.**

LEFT: A Spetsnaz Spetsrota counter-terrorist soldier from the Felixdzerzhinsky Division delivers a high kick to the throat of a member of the OPFOR as team members follow through behind during an exercise in the unit's training village.

unarmed combat in the armed forces of the world. For by the 20th century, military technology in both West and East had rendered the close-in skills of the individual warrior largely redundant. Spears, bows, crossbows, gunpowder, cannons, rifles, explosives, artillery, rockets, combat aircraft: the distance at which one could deliver death and destruction inexorably expanded and made unarmed fighting ability seem increasingly crude and unnecessary. During the Korean War, for example, North Korean units of martial arts experts were sent against the allied lines only to be mown down hundreds of metres from their targets by heavy machine-guns and artillery shells. Thus a British Army recruit of around this time would receive little or no training in unarmed combat, it was simply not necessary (or so it was believed).

Yet against this pattern of reduction, unarmed combat started to become more infused into the culture of world-wide special forces, the elite units with lethal skills which flourished in the 20th century's politically and strategically complex war zones.

UNARMED ASSASSINATION TECHNIQUES

For units such as the SOE and Commandos, unarmed assassination techniques became essential parts of their operational effectiveness. US Special Forces in Vietnam between 1963 and 1973 continued such a prioritisation on deadly unarmed force in the jungles of South-East Asia, as did the Korean forces in the same conflict who dispatched many Viet Cong insurgents with single lethal blows to the neck or head. To this day it is the Special Forces who excel more than most military units in unarmed combat, though the quality and quantity of training varies tremendously between forces and individual units, often being dependent on the skills of certain personnel and their willingness to impart their knowledge.

This is true for almost all military units around the world, apart from those fortunate enough (like the South Koreans and Israelis) to have martial arts as part of core training. One thing is apparent however. Unarmed combat remains an essential part of the soldier's combat authority.

Although unarmed combat in a military context learns many lessons from the monks' art of kung fu, which is

COLONEL REX APPLEGATE

The name Colonel Rex Applegate is synonymous with American military training in unarmed combat. He was very frank about what the aim of this training was – learning how to remove an enemy soldier permanently from the war. He said: 'Any hold should be regarded as a means of getting a man into a position where it will be easier to kill him and not as a means to keep him captive. The whole idea of releasing yourself from a hold or in applying one is to be able to kill. The disengaging move should form the beginning of an attack.'

Applegate, who died in 1998, aged 84, had a rich pedigree. He was born in Oregon on 21 June 1914 and his family roots went back to the American Revolution and the pioneering trek on the Oregon Trail. He was an expert marksman and hunter in his youth, inspired by his uncle, Gus Peret, a renowned exhibition shooter and professional hunter.

Applegate graduated from Oregon University in 1940 with a degree in business administration. As a member of the Reserve Officer Training Corps, he was commissioned as a second lieutenant in the US Army Reserve.

He was a big bear of a man, and it was partly because of his size – partly too because of his taste for contact sports and his father's experience as a lawman – that he was assigned to the 209th Military Police Company. This is where the war found him when America joined World War II in 1941. By the next year he was helping to set up schools for close combat fighting with and without weapons. Throughout the war Applegate masterminded the Office of Strategic Services' training and clandestine missions.

In 1945, Applegate moved into the private sector but maintained his interest in security. He continued to follow close combat strategy during the Korean War in the 1950s and worked with the Mexican police and army in the 60s.

By the 1970s he was semi-retired and working as a consultant. His three books – *Kill or Get Killed*, *Riot Control* and *Scouting and Patrolling* – are used worldwide by the military and the police. Applegate studied with all the notable figures of his era and also served for a time as one of President Franklin D. Roosevelt's personal bodyguards. In his last years, he was an adviser to the US Department of Defense, federal law enforcement officers and to foreign police and military services.

basically a form of self-defence, its combative scope reaches far beyond self-defence. The ideal for self-defence techniques is that they should repel an attack, if they can, without so much as causing injury to the attacker. By contrast, military unarmed combat techniques aim at inflicting bodily damage on the opponent, without any worries over risking his life. The main purpose is always to inflict as much damage as quickly as possible and at the same time

BELOW: Most elite forces include martial arts in their training programmes, although the quality and quantity of training varies widely. The main influences are karate, kung fu, taekwondo and ju-jitsu, the latter's pragmatic techniques making it a particularly popular combat form.

receive the bare minimum in return. In most cases killing the opponent will be the only militarily sound objective.

Combat sports, such as boxing under the Marquis of Queensberry rules, forbid a long list of fouls – such as blows to the testicles – but these have to be regarded as perfectly acceptable, even as indispensable, moves in military unarmed combat. A soldier is trained to hit an opponent at his weakest points. An eventual real-life opponent is sure to attack the soldier's own weakest points if given a chance, and unlike a boxer a soldier is thoroughly trained in defending them.

There is nothing personal is this. It is just part of a soldier's job to learn how to kill or maim enemy soldiers,

and unarmed combat training means learning how to kill or maim with your hands. Long before being introduced to unarmed combat, a soldier will already have mastered the most important principle of any military conflict – do not personalise the enemy. In a fight, trained soldiers do not see enemy faces as the faces of individuals. What they learn to see is a target. In the case of hand-to-hand combat, they learn to see a whole collection of vital bodily target points. Often the best way of achieving this state of mind is to focus attention away from the opponent's face and to concentrate on the point just below the attacker's collarbone. This point of attention enables the defender to have

ABOVE: Soldiers from the Spetsnaz, the Soviet special forces, training in unarmed combat techniques, using hands and feet to learn to kill or cripple an opponent. They are taught where to strike to be most effective. Their training regime is notoriously tough and intense.

a peripheral overview of all the attacker's limb and body movements, making the defender sensitive to all hostile movements in advance of their final delivery and also stopping the defender becoming mesmerised by the opponent's facial expressions or words. It also enables the defender quickly to sense opportunities for attack. By maintaining a neutral (though aggressive) attitude towards

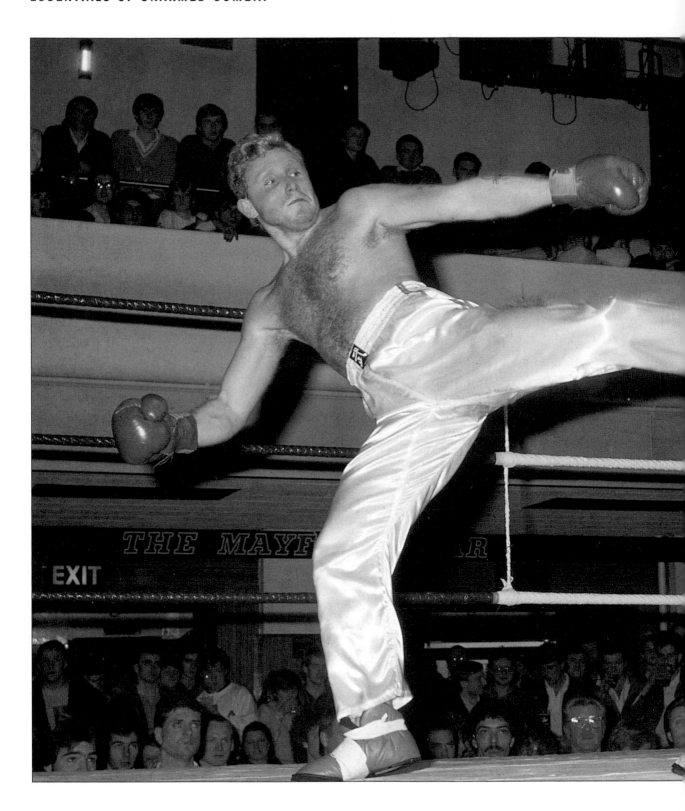

LEFT: Kick boxing, seen here at the York Hall in east London's Bethnal Green district, is becoming increasingly popular. It is a combination of muay thai and karate. Kick boxing techniques are adapted to suit elite unit requirements.

any attacker, the defender is less likely to be overcome by fear or intimidation if the attacker is of greater size than him. Ideally the defender should in no way predict the outcome of the fight but rather use his confidence and techniques as and when the targets present themselves.

Although kicking a man when he is down, gouging out his eyes and kicking him in the testicles does not appeal to most fair-minded people, these are an absolute necessity in unarmed combat with an enemy soldier. Ruthlessness is the intention, combined with speed and brutality. In this type of fighting, it does not matter much what is done so long as it is done fast and as if your life depends on it – because it probably does. Surprise and speed are the two chief elements. This applies as much to the individual as it does to the strategy of armies. The intention is to attack, not simply defend. Attack should be such that each blow will be a step toward nullifying the danger of the enemy. Each attack is also a defence.

Using unarmed combat skills in a military context is therefore something very different from practising them as a sport, or learning them to protect yourself from street fighters. A soldier training to attack enemy soldiers does not concern himself with delicate questions about how far he can go in a fight without breaking the law. Either the enemy dies or he does, and his best chance of staying alive begins with ruthless training.

If you are in a state of war, the aim will most likely be to kill an opponent, and to kill him as quickly as possible. A prisoner is a handicap and a source of danger if a soldier is without weapons.

REALISM IN UNARMED COMBAT

Military training in unarmed combat is starkly realistic, and this sets it well apart from most of what meets the public eye under the title of martial arts.

Many recreational unarmed combat techniques are useful only as a means of restraint. Instructors often rely on practice routines in which an opponent remains completely passive, without movement, enabling the student to apply a hold. Anyone applying this type of combat training cannot expect to get away without injury to himself in a real-life situation. Too many people have

ABOVE: US Army Rangers practise how to lure an opponent into believing the captured soldier is totally submissive before he mounts a counter attack. Note the arms raised in mock surrender before a chopping blow to the back of the head is delivered.

They would not come out alive, let alone unscathed, if their films were reality. Chuck Norris, Jackie Chan and other heroes of the big screen may be great martial artists, but the fact is they would not last a moment with the sort of adversity they all encounter in their films.

The popularity of kung fu and action films originates from a combination of trends in the 1970s – the discovery of Zen among the young, the star presence of Bruce Lee and the compulsive attraction of his brutal fighting, plus the kicks audiences got out of seeing kicks. It's the escapism they enjoy. Unarmed combat in the military is far removed from the celluloid version of fighting.

WEAPONS OF OPPORTUNITY

There is nothing pure about military hand-to-hand combat, and so it doesn't even have to be unarmed. Anything that can be held in a hand and used to damage or destroy the opponent is a legitimate accessory to the soldier's other weapons – his hands, feet, knees, shoulders, elbows, clawing fingers, butting head and biting teeth. A battlefield can contain a variety of objects that can be picked up and used as a weapon. A soldier's resourcefulness and imagination are only his limitations. Here are some examples of objects that are typically available.

The entrenching tool (E-tool) is an excellent weapon, especially when sharpened. It can be used to block and strike an enemy and its sharp edges can be used to slash the enemy's neck and throat area.

A helmet can also be used to strike the enemy's unprotected head and face. Tent poles and pins are useful and can be used as a knife substitute for the throat and groin areas. Any sharp, hard object – say a broken tree limb, stick, iron rod or pipe – can be used in the same manner as tent poles and pins.

A belt is useful for blocking hand attacks. Once the attack is blocked, it can be used in the follow up for garrotting. Tent guide lines, boot laces and communication wires can also be used to garrotte an opponent.

The idea of pointing a finger into a man's back to simulate a gun barrel is fine, providing the soldier bends the finger and places the knuckle there to fake a gun barrel convincingly.

been given the impression that such methods of combat provide a magical means of subduing an opponent, without personal risk.

Another obstacle to realistic thinking about unarmed combat is cinema. In reality, fighting hand-to-hand is nothing like the stuff of movies. Bruce Willis, Sly Stallone, Harrison Ford and Arnold Swarzenegger could only survive the sort of fantasy fights they have in their films.

BODY RESPONSE TO EXTREME STRESS

One of the major challenges of any unarmed combat training programme is to give the soldier the strength of mind to deal with the acute shock that often accompanies an actual life-threatening situation. All human beings are born with the physiological fight or flight mechanism, the reactive capacity to alter muscular, hormonal and mental states under extreme stress to enable us to respond to a threat with greater physical force. Yet this mechanism is an ancient one, born of a prehistoric time when human beings had to face death or danger every day. In modern society we have grown unaccustomed to dealing with such threats. Consequently, when we are placed in a situation of extreme stress the biological changes which occur can actually deprive us of physical initiative rather than enable it.

When faced with a stressful situation (known medically as a stressor), the brain's hypothalamus is quickly activated and sets in train a series of hormonal reactions which lead to the release of adrenaline and noradrenaline from the adrenal medulla into the bloodstream. This produces an increase in respiration, heart rate and blood pressure and draws blood away from surface vessels and the brain and diverts it to the muscles to provide them with more sugar and oxygen. The liver also starts to release stored glucose to fuel this process. Following this initial shock reaction, the body attempts to stabilise itself in adjustment to the situation and adrenal levels dip back towards normal, though the individual remains highly motivated.

The psychological effect of the stress reaction can be extremely debilitating as well as empowering. With the blood draining to the muscles there is the danger of going into shock and being mentally paralysed by the unfamiliar sensations occurring in the body. Confusion, anxiety and physical weakness can thus occur, and instead of acquiring greater physical strength the individual can psychologically retreat from the stressor and consequently lose contact with the reality of their plight. In unarmed combat training, they should be just enough real danger present to provoke the adrenal stress reaction. As the soldier becomes more accustomed to continuing the fight under such conditions, then the likelihood of him experiencing paralysis in a life-threatening situation becomes dramatically reduced.

FIGHTING AT CLOSE QUARTERS

Karate experts giving an exhibition of their skill or kung fu artists performing in a film may leave you with an impression that unarmed combat is something that happens at the intermediate range - the distance from which a professional boxer throws a punch, or a taekwondo champion delivers a kick. In reality, though, most of the unarmed combat a soldier actually experiences will occur in close grappling range, and it will involve joint manipulation, choking, gouging and ripping techniques.

Soldiers are not trained to seek this distance, it just happens to be the most likely one in which they will find themselves. The ideal fighting distance is in quite the opposite direction, beyond the intermediate and well outside of the reach of any enemy soldier's arm - the farther away the better. The human body's natural centre of gravity is centred in the waist about three inches below the navel and not the shoulders (men in the West tend to use their shoulders as the focus of movement whereas in the East men tend to move more naturally from the hips). For the most stable fighting posture, the soldier should train himself to move, kick and strike with the waist as the centre of power and balance. If this is achieved, then there is much less of a likelihood of falling to ground in a combat situation.

The more normal - more distant - fighting involves firearms, usually from a very long range. The impression our televisions screens have given us in many of the recent conflicts around the world, such as the Iraq-Iran war, the Gulf War and the Pakistan–India troubles, is perfectly accurate - the more firepower armies have, the more they are inclined to fight each other from distances of tens, even hundreds of miles, with air strikes, missiles and long-range artillery.

Fighting within grappling distance leaves little or no room to manoeuvre; so a basic first lesson of unarmed combat for soldiers is to keep their distance if they can - keep their adversary at arm's length. A second basic lesson is never go to ground with him, if they can help it. If a soldier does find himself on the ground then this means getting too close to his opponent, with little room to work, and no room to see what the opponent is up to.

But soldiers do fall; so they are taught to fall properly, in hour upon hour of practice. As there is a big difference between falling on mats and falling on uneven, rocky ground, however, the emphasis is on training soldiers to stay on their feet.

The soldiers are taught that, once on the ground, they should never stop trying to get into a position that will allow them to return to their feet. And they are taught that it is not necessary to follow an opponent to the ground once he has been put there. In fact, the soldier's feet are the best weapons to finish him when he is down. Going to ground and remaining immobile, a soldier is at his enemy's mercy and vulnerable to attack from the opponent's feet, bayonet or any other weapon.

Instinctive reaction is absolutely vital if a soldier is to acquit himself competently in a fighting scenario. In actual combat the forces of stress, fear and excitement combine to deprive a fighter of much of his capacity for rational or decisive thought. In such situations the body responds by resorting to more instinctive physical actions. Effective

ABOVE: Springing from behind a tree, a soldier applies a suffocating head lock to an unwary patrolling infantryman. The grip around the neck could be turned into a rapid neck-break, snapping the shoulders back and impacting on the vertebra at the top of the spine.

unarmed combat training aims to give the soldier a body of techniques which have been repeated so often that they form a part of this instinctive response mechanism during any actual combat situation. Rational thought is far too slow for the split second shifts of an unarmed encounter, so a simple but powerful repertoire of techniques which can be delivered as a matter of reflex is vital.

The key to generating this response mechanism lies in the nature of the training. In any situation, the human mind's first reaction is to search through its 'files' of experience to see whether the current task or demand matches anything which has happened in the past and can form the experiential basis for a response. If a situation is unique, such as a fight (for one who is not accustomed to fighting), the brain can find no previous model and can

instead go into paralysis of decision. Hard, realistic training in unarmed combat essentially gives the soldier that mental model to respond to an actual fight situation with plenty of mental references of how it feels to defend oneself. Repeating techniques time and time again, and increasing the power with which they are delivered to accustom the soldier to actually being in danger, means that in a life threatening environment defensive techniques are a matter of reflex and the shock of the experience of combat is much reduced.

BELOW: Sometimes kicking an opponent in the ribs is the most effective way of countering an attack. Disarming an opponent with a gun can be a dangerous course of action and often the element of surprise by simply kicking out can be effective.

RUSSIAN MILITARY MARTIAL ARTS

The history of Russian/Soviet military martial arts is as fascinating as it is complex. Prior to the October Revolution of 1917, Russia had a multitude of regional and ethnic martial arts which are today collectively known as Russian Martial Art (RMA). From several millennia before the birth of Christ to roughly the 6th century AD, RMA was a varied tribal practice amongst Slavic warrior communities, used in both internal and inter-tribe competitions and also in the reality of tribal warfare. The combat skills were passed from father to son, martial hereditary maintaining and also developing the corpus of techniques over the centuries. This was to be valuable, for from the 6th century AD, Russian tribes came more under attack from northern and western invaders, though the invaders' first hand accounts of this time indicate that their opponents were ferocious hand-to-hand fighters. From the 9th century, however, metallurgical advances were starting to affect the course of RMA development. Improved swords, spears and armour led to the need for more decisive hand-to-hand techniques which could be used to tackle even armed opponents. Another, perhaps more profound influence on RMA, was the Mongol occupation of Russia initiated by Batu Khan in 1237, an occupation which remained until the late 15th century.

Two centuries after the Mongol occupation, RMA went into something of a decline. The influence of less sophisticated martial traditions from the West and the eventual introduction of firearms meant a steady degrading of RMA authority and skills, though it remained as a persistent cultural presence throughout Russia into the twentieth century.

The revolution of 1917 signalled a major shift in the fortunes and direction of RMA in Russia. Following the establishment of the Bolshevik government, the communist regime set out to iron flat the Soviet Union's variegated cultural traditions and create a homogenous socialist landscape. RMA was no exception to this policy, and in 1918 Lenin founded an organisation under one Comrade Vorosilov to research Russian and foreign martial arts systems and create an integrated military combat form standardised throughout the USSR. Teams of investigators travelled throughout the Soviet Union, Mongolia, China, India, Japan, Africa and Europe and built up a massive profile of martial techniques and traditions. Once this was pooled back in Vorosilov's HQ, 25 Russian unarmed combat styles were brought together with karate, judo and other defensive forms into a tiered structure of martial art skills to be taught to the military.

The top tier was occupied by the Soviet Close-Quarters Combat (CQC) programme. Taught only to Special Forces soldiers and Secret Police units, CQC was a highly secret selection of lethal unarmed techniques for assassination, combat killing and torture, techniques which kept close to the original teachings of RMA despite the Soviet attempts to deny this. Emphasis was placed on techniques such as strangulation and fatal strikes, these being thoroughly tested in the Russo-Japanese War and World War I. Below CQC was Soviet Police Subject and Crowd Control Tactics (CCT). CCT provided good restraint skills using locks, pressure point holds and compliance-generating kicks and strikes. Lastly, there was a general level of martial art instruction to be given to all Soviet army units, which was actually more geared to competitive sporting use than rigorous unarmed combat skills.

Thus the Soviet authorities assimilated RMA into their ideological structure while also preventing the total dissemination of lethal unarmed knowledge. The new forms were collectively gathered into a combat style known as Sambo, and acronym standing for Samozashchitya Bez Oruzhiya, meaning self-protection without weapons. Sambo generally fell into two categories: Sport Sambo and Combat Sambo, and almost all Russian military personnel would encounter its techniques in one form or another, though often without the lethality of training that Special Forces soldiers received. For there was another form of Sambo known as Combat Sambo Spetsnaz. This is essentially the repository of genuine RMA techniques, the Sambo reference in its title being more to placate outside curiosity. Its techniques were taught in absolute secrecy, and it was often known simply as The System by those who practised it. It is now the province of Russia's elite Spetsnaz special forces units and of key personnel in Russian institutions such as the Ministry of Internal Affairs, Ministry of Defence, MVD Special units, VDV Paratrooper and OMON units, certain Russian Marine squads and other specialists. Slowly, the techniques of Combat Sambo Spetsnaz are becoming known to the outside world. Yet while there are now many in the West who claim themselves as Sambo instructors, some being former Soviet Army personnel, few outside Russia actually have knowledge of the full scope, potential and techniques of Sambo as derived from the ancient RMA.

The Martial Arts Heritage

Unarmed combat is the oldest form of fighting known to man. As human society developed, so did its methods of war, but no matter how technical or scientific fighting becomes, there will always be hand-to-hand struggle.

A soldier – especially a special forces soldier – can easily find himself in an empty-hand fight as a result of weapons failure, depleted ammunition, or unsuccessful escape and evasion attempts. To prevail, he needs to be fully trained in the uses of weapons that are always at his disposal, never jam and never run out of ammo – his hands and feet. Properly used, they will stop an attacker dead in his tracks.

The special forces soldier is heavily armed with an array of weapons specific to his mission. Sometimes he will engage the enemy only as a last resort, especially if his mission is to gather intelligence without leaving any trace of having been there. Or he will use unarmed combat in the unlikely occurrence of his weapons failing, or during an escape and evasion attempt.

LEFT: Egyptian Army Rangers put on a dramatic exhibition of combat moves. Unarmed combat remains an essential part of a soldier's combat authority and can provide invaluable skills in the unlikely event of a weapons failure.

ABOVE: Members of Moscow's Alpha Force practise their throwing and falling techniques at a secret training centre.

When modern weapons do fail to stop the opponent, soldiers must rely on their unarmed combat skills – they are literally the last line of defence. These techniques show a soldier how to fight without the use of firearms, knives, or other conventional weapons. They are designed for use when those weapons have been lost (a situation which should be avoided at all costs) or when the use of firearms is undesirable for fear of raising an alarm. In special forces operations, the need for silent infiltration may make unarmed combat a first option for combat, if combat there is to be. In peace-keeping situations, soldiers always see unarmed combat as the first option, using weapons only in extreme cases. They would rather capture someone with their bare hands than maim or kill.

WORLD WAR II COMMANDOS

One of the first commando instructors to give a high priority to military training in unarmed combat was William Ewart Fairbairn, a British Army officer who, with his partner Major William Sykes, invented the Fairbairn-Sykes double-edged fighting knife. Both had served for many years with the Shanghai police before being recruited during World War II to train members of the Royal Commandos, as well as agents of the Office of Strategic Services and Special Operations Executive.

Fairbairn was an expert in weapons instruction. He also demanded proficiency in unarmed fighting skills. Why did Fairbairn consider martial arts training to be so important for special forces? One of his students, George Langelaan, provides the answer in his classic book, now long out of print, about the Special Operations Executive, *No Colours of Crest*.

RIGHT: Japanese woodblock print of Samurai-Yoshitune at the battle of Yoshima. Many combat moves derive from Oriental martial arts – the study of martial arts provided self-confidence and a sense of physical power to many soldiers.

'Fairbairn gave us more and more self-confidence which gradually grew into a sense of physical power and superiority that few men ever acquire,' wrote Langelaan. 'By the time we finished our training, I would have willingly tackled any man, whatever his strength, size or ability. He taught us to face the possibility of a fight without the slightest tremor of apprehension, a state of mind which very few professional boxers ever enjoy and which so often means more than half the battle. Strange as it may seem, it is understandable when a man knows for certain that he can hurt, maul, injure or even kill with the greatest of ease and that during every split second or a fight, he has not one but a dozen different openings, different possibilities to choose from.'

During World War II, in fact, although several countries introduced elements of Japanese martial arts into their hand-to-hand combat training, very few soldiers received this kind of training, and scouting patrols were generally not good at unarmed combat or capturing prisoners. They relied on their weapons. Scouts with the right training, however, engaged in unarmed fighting on bold raids. The unexpected, silent attack on the enemy, the unforeseen encounter right in his own territory often produced dramatic results.

THE LEGACY OF KUNG FU

Military instructors ever since William Fairbairn's day have taught five fundamentals as the basis for unarmed combat. They are:

1 making full use of any available weapon;
2 attacking aggressively by using maximum strength against the enemy's weakest point;
3 maintaining balance while destroying an opponent's;
4 using the opponent's momentum to advantage;
5 learning each phase of all the movements precisely and accurately before attaining speed through constant practise.

These principles are imbedded in the many Oriental martial arts that have inspired Western military training in unarmed combat since the 1940s and which invaded the West as sport and spectacle in the second half of the 20th century. Among these is the oldest surviving discipline of unarmed combat taught – kung fu, or Chinese boxing. Even though it has a strong non-military streak, its influence on other styles makes it a direct ancestor of most of the techniques Western armed forces have adopted since World War II to improve hand-to-hand combat training.

To understand martial arts, a fundamental distinction must be made. Pure martial arts tend to fall into one of two categories: internal or external, alternatively known as hard and soft styles. An external, hard style is one which focuses almost exclusively on meeting an attacker's physical force with an equal or greater force. Training in such martial arts, including karate, muay thai (Thai kickboxing) and judo, is usually punishing, and develops the individual to use kicks, punches and strikes with maximum power while also conditioning his or her body to absorb blows and blocks without succumbing to pain. Mentally, the hard arts focus on strength of spirit and ferocity in the attack. By contrast, the internal arts, tai chi chuan, pa kua and hsing-i being good examples, concentrate less upon meeting force with force and more on yielding to attack and using the attacker's own momentum to defeat him. The internal styles concentrate more on evasion and relaxed, flowing movements. Thus if an attacker threw a punch at a karate fighter, the blow would probably be stopped hard by a forearm block and countered with a violent return blow to the assailant's vulnerable points. Yet if a practitioner of the soft arts was defending against the same blow, the punching arm would probably be guided past the body with a simple deflecting action and the attacker then thrown using his own forward momentum against him.

The differences between the hard and soft styles extend to attitude: the soft styles often give more focus to the martial art as a spiritual practice and a way of self-discovery. Yet the division between the internal and external martial arts is not watertight, and especially since the introduction of Zen into Western culture in the early 20th century most hard martial arts have taken soft philosophies into their practice and outlook (though the reverse is rarely true). But in considering the following kung fu styles, it is worth remembering the fundamental distinction between styles.

Chinese monks in the northern province of Honan, where lies the legendary Shaolin temple, developed kung fu as a method of self-defence (for example, against thieves and nomad tribes given to temple-raiding) and as a form of exercise to promote good health. This philosophy of self-defence and healthful exercise still prevails in kung fu. The system developed over a period of centuries through trial and error. Then for more centuries it remained basically unchanged, although a huge range of different styles have now evolved. Many thousands of kung fu styles exist in Asia today.

The monks adapted this style in turn from other martial-art forms. No region of the world is without its own (in most cases largely forgotten) history of ritualised fighting, but some traditions become more formalised and more widely taught than others. The ancestors of kung fu may include one of these – the ancient Greek art of pankration, introduced to Asia by the invading armies of Alexander the Great in the 4th century BC, and Graeco-Roman wrestling may have been another influence.

The most direct foreign influence on kung fu is thought to have come from India, through the legendary Buddhist monk, Bodhidharma. He crossed the Himalayas on foot to arrive at a run-down monastery whose monks were in a poor state of health. Through his instruction, the monks learned a series of health-giving exercises based on Indian systems of yoga that returned them to full health and vitality. These exercises developed into the 18 hands of Lo-Han and are the foundation of Shaolin temple boxing.

LEFT: The influence of Oriental culture is still prevalent in combat fighting. Martial arts fall into two categories: internal and external, also known as hard and soft styles. These are represented by the antagonistic yet complementary opposites of the Chinese *yin* and *yang* symbols.

ABOVE: Egyptian special forces practise locks and constrictions. They need to be careful when applying pressure on each other as certain techniques can render an opponent unconscious instantly.

BODHIDHARMA

The life of Bodhidharma is clouded by myth and contradiction, yet he is venerated throughout the world not only as one of the first patriarchs of Zen Buddhism, but also a founding father of the martial arts. The legend goes that Bodhidharma was born in Kanchipuram near Madras, and in AD 520 he journeyed to China, first to the city of Kuang were he met Emperor Wu Ti, then staying at the Shaolin monastery at Songshan. There he is reputed to have established a meditative style of Buddhism, which became Zen, and also Shaolin Temple boxing, the cornerstone of kung fu and, arguably, many other Far Eastern martial arts. This is not the same as saying the Bodhidharma founded systems of unarmed combat; they were already in place by the time of his arrival. What he did bring, however, was the synthesis of martial arts and Eastern spirituality which associated unarmed combat skills with self-development, humility and non-aggression.

And yet, for all his influence it is difficult to know exactly what to attribute to this enigmatic figure. Apart from an eyewitness record of him written by Yang Hsuan-chih in AD 547, no other contemporary references exist, even in the Shaolin monks' writings. Only some 500 years later do lengthy texts on Bodhidharma emerge, though the hiatus may be explained by the fact that the initially heretical status and anti-textual attitude of Chan Buddhism did not lend itself to the production and preservation of scriptural or personal accounts. Concerning Bodhidharma's legacy to the martial arts, there is even greater uncertainty. The sophisticated development of unarmed combat skills in the Far East after Bodhidharma's time means that his direct influence on actual technique and style is almost entirely lost. Yet regardless of issues of historical accuracy, Bodhidharma's iconic presentation of how the martial artist should be and behave has undoubtedly influenced the formation of the martial arts across the centuries.

Kung fu has evolved into five major styles – called Hung, Choy, Mok (or Monk), Lau and Li after their creators. Each is based on the movements of an animal – the tiger, crane, leopard, snake or dragon.

One of the most popular styles of kung fu today is wing chun, meaning 'beautiful spring-time'. Its popularity stems from the fact that it was invented by a woman and it needs only a minimum exertion of force to do the maximum amount of work. The style started with a Shaolin nun, Ng Mui, who taught it to a young village girl, Yim Wing Chun. Being of slight build, Yim Wing Chun thought Ng Mui's style relied too heavily on power techniques more suited to a man; so she developed her own style and dedicated it to the Buddhist nun but named it after herself.

The modern-day exponent of the style was the late grand master, Yip Man. One of the most famous students of wing chun was Bruce Lee. Most of wing chun is based on hand manoeuvres and subtle, shifting footwork. Very few kicks are used and the few that are used are aimed below the waist. The art of wing chun is based on economy of movement, emphasising hand techniques to make use of the opponent's force to strengthen the practitioner's counter-attack. Wing chun can be very useful in a combat situation for this very reason.

KUNG FU STYLES

Tai chi chuan is an 'internal style' of kung fu founded by the Taoist mystic, Chang San-Feng in the 14th century. Legend has it that Chang San-Feng lived in the mountains

where he brewed a hypnotic drink. After drinking the brew he fell into a deep sleep and dreamed of a series of fighting manoeuvres all based on a complete yielding to attack. When he woke two days later, he put into practice everything he had dreamt. The practice consisted of a slow-motion exercise that never stopped. Each movement slipped into the next in an ever-continuing circle. Chang San-Feng passed on his kung fu style to a disciple, Chen Chia Kou, some years later, and the Chen family kept the secret of the form for more than 400 years. A descendant elaborated the exercises and the style eventually split into two branches. The other branch became the yang style that is popular in the West today.

Pa-kua is one of the oldest forms of kung fu, possibly 5,000 years old and is another internal system. Pa-kua means 'eight trigrams'. The style is based on the premise that if you can defend yourself at the eight major compass points covered by the trigrams you will be fully protected from attack. The art has many open-palm strikes and the foot-work is based on the circle. Students mount their attacks in twisting, spiralling movements. The twist is done from the waist and generates immense power.

Hsing-i is a third internal style. It was invented by a general named Yueh Fei in the 12th century and is sometimes known as Chinese mind boxing. The movements are very graceful, and the art stresses the yin-yang principle of complementary opposites, hard and soft.

The praying mantis style was invented by a Chinese boxer named Wong Long. After being constantly beaten by fighters from other styles, he retired to meditate. One day, sitting in a temple garden, he noticed a grasshopper and a praying mantis locked in battle and he observed that the mantis was fighting in a definite pattern. Facing a much larger and heavier opponent, the mantis would make lightning strikes with its claw-like front limbs, then beat a hasty retreat out of harm's way when the grasshopper retaliated. Fascinated, Wong Long captured the mantis and took it home with him. There he examined the insect's every move by prodding the poor thing with a twig. He then devised a system

LEFT: Here karate experts give a demonstration of their skills. Martial arts training in the military teaches the soldier how to face a combat situation without fear or apprehension: a critical state of mind when facing an enemy.

LEFT: British Army recruits practise methods of releasing themselves from leg holds during unarmed combat training. Most kicks are directed below the waist to avoid the danger of the leg being grabbed.

ABOVE: A soldier (right) makes an open-handed attack to the eyes as a way of breaking his training partner's strong collar grip. His left hand is retracted ready for a strong follow-up punch.

of fighting derived from the mantis's movements and went back to do battle with the fighters from other systems. So successful was he that he named his new style after the insect.

Bok hok pai, otherwise known as 'the white crane', was invented by Tibetan lamas and was at one time reserved for the use of the elite corps of bodyguards that protected the emperor of China. This style came into being after a lama saw a fight between a white crane and an ape. The lama noticed that as the ape rushed into the attack, the crane would defend by evading and then retaliate with its wings. The lama put together eight techniques from the crane's natural movements and incorporated them with the ape's footwork and grabbing manoeuvres. White crane techniques exist in many other styles of kung fu.

Hung gar is an adaptation of the Shaolin tiger system, but it also has aspects of white crane. It is characterised by low, wide stances that produce strong solid legs. This low stance is known as the horse stance, or ma pu. Hung gar is a strong, hard kung fu style, containing a powerful thrust punch which exponents maintain always results in a knock out. Today's unarmed combat style most closely derives from hung gar which stresses close-quarter fighting methods.

Choy lee fut originated with Chan Heung. It began as a secret combat training method for forming the Chinese rebels into a fighting force during the Opium Wars of the 19th century. The power source is the waist. Both high and low kicks are involved in the execution of its techniques. This long-range system of boxing involves many deceptive and elusive foot manoeuvres. The hand techniques

THE SHAOLIN TEMPLE

Situated on the western slopes of the Songshan mountains in Honan Province, the Shaolin Temple is a cultural landmark not only for its fundamental involvement in the expansion of Buddhist theology, but also for its contribution to the martial arts. It was founded in AD 495 at the order of Emperor Hsiao-wen for the Indian monk Batuo, and became a focal point for Buddhist spirituality and the translation of Indian scripture into Chinese. Bodhidharma himself visited the temple in the 6th century, laying the meditative foundations for what would become Zen Buddhism (known as Chan Buddhism in China) and also instructing the monks in elemental techniques of the martial arts. During the 7th century, Tang Dynasty emperor Tai Tsung gave the Temple permission to raise a force of 500 monk soldiers (about a third of the Temple's manpower) after coming to the Emperor's assistance in a time of political unrest. Consequently, the new martial sanction and Bodhidharma's earlier influence came together in an astonishing school of unarmed combat and spirituality. Combat training was hard and realist, the spirituality humble and devout. In the 17th century, the Temple was burnt down on the orders of Ching Dynasty emperor Kang-Hsi who feared the fighting skills present in the Temple (even though the Shaolin monks had fought for him in 1674). The surviving monks scattered throughout various monasteries and employment. The Temple was extensively rebuilt following Kang Hsi's reign, but gradually its martial and spiritual practice declined and ceased in 1928. Today, the Shaolin name is continued in hundreds of martial schools throughout China, though only a few authentically continue the traditions established over 1300 years ago.

ABOVE: Egyptian special forces perform a sequence of block-and-counter manoeuvres. This training in unarmed combat skills forms an integral part of each recruit's military training.

incorporate hooks and uppercuts, back-fists and round-house punches, all delivered with devastating force.

THE JAPANESE INFLUENCE

Japan has had a more direct influence on unarmed combat training than China. Ju-jitsu, the 'art of flexibility', was one of the first Japanese arts to be recognised in the West. Its origins reach beyond the 10th century. Around the 12th century, the Japanese became interested in kung fu and adapted ju-jitsu to take in Chinese ideas.

It is ju-jitsu – from the outset an art practised by soldiers rather than monks – with its vast range of locks, holds and strangulation techniques, that the armed forces of many countries made the foundation for their unarmed combat training. Its flexibility lends itself to the demands of the modern soldier – its long-range kicks and strikes, close-in grappling, throws, hand locks and attacks to the body's pressure points all have military application.

Ju-jitsu does not include many blows to the head or body. This stems from medieval times, when the enemy would be a soldier wearing protective armour and a helmet. The arms and legs might be the only exposed

RIGHT: A French parachute soldier executes a powerful shoulder throw on his comrade during training. Note that the thrower still retains control of his opponent's arm to prevent him fighting back from the floor.

targets on such an adversary, hence the concentration on locks and selective strikes to the joints.

Ju-jitsu was developed by Japanese Samurai warriors in specialist schools that taught archery, sword-fighting, strategy and horsemanship, as well as unarmed combat tactics. Unarmed combat was considered a last resort for the warrior who might have lost his weapon or been taken by surprise with his sword sheathed. It was also useful when a valuable prisoner was to be taken alive for his ransom value. The Samurai agenda was focused on dominating enemies; the kung fu monk was focused on physical

ABOVE: US Army troops during a session spent learning throws and break falls. Military clothing, being robustly made, makes it ideal for executing throws, as civilian clothing often simply tears when extreme force is applied to it.

culture. Consequently, ju-jitsu developed as a quicker, easier-to-learn style of fighting than kung fu. For this reason, it provides many practical techniques for training today's special forces soldier.

Ju-jitsu's sporting form, judo, has been used as a method for training law enforcement officers in arrest and hold techniques. Judo was the brainchild of Jigoro Kano (1860–1938), who in the 1880s sought to develop a system of physical exercise. After attending several ju-jitsu schools he adopted the best principles of each ju-jitsu system and called it judo, which, literally translated, means 'gentle way'. Kano's interpretation of the discipline, however, was 'maximum efficiency'. It became the first martial art in the

Olympic Games in 1964. Kano established a school called Kodokan for the study of judo and for its application to unarmed combat. Kano's philosophy applies perfectly to the world's military forces:

'Judo is the means of understanding the way to make the most effective use of both physical and spiritual power and strength. By devoted practice and rigid discipline, in an effort to obtain perfection in attacking and defending, it refines the body and soul and helps instil the spiritual essence in judo into every part of one's very being. In this way, it is possible to perfect oneself and contribute something worthwhile to the world.' Jiguro Kano

Many of today's unarmed military combat methods originate from judo. What a soldier is taught in unarmed combat must be simple – he must be able to execute it with great speed. He must practice it intensively until he is able to react instinctively in an unarmed combat situation with the few blows, kick and releases that are needed for the task at hand. Judo is a firm grounding for this.

KARATE

Karate, which means 'empty hand', began on the Japanese island of Okinawa and was greatly influenced by Chinese combat methods and systems. Karate was first introduced into Japan by a mild-mannered Okinawan schoolmaster, Gichin Funakoshi, an expert in the punching and kicking arts of his island homeland, where his teacher was a great master named Azato.

Funakoshi put on a karate display for the Emperor of Japan who was so impressed that he asked him to stay in Tokyo and teach his art more widely. Very soon the schoolteacher became the idol of Japanese martial arts circles. He opened his first school or 'dojo' (training house) in Tokyo. His pen name when he wrote poetry was Shoto and the club was known as Shotokan ('kan' means club).

In the years that followed Funakoshi's arrival in Japan, several other styles were introduced into the country by other Okinawan masters. By the 1930s most leading Japanese universities had thriving karate clubs. Funakoshi's son, Yoshitaka, became something of a driving force behind his father's club and it is to him that the famous 'mawashi geri' or roundhouse kick is credited. Yoshitaka introduced new elements to the art, until gradually karate lost some of its distinctive Okinawan features. Within quite a short time

great rivalries grew up between students of different styles. Practitioners of the art broke away to form new styles more attuned to their own ways of thinking, and karate began to fragment.

After World War II karate was banned in Japan by the American forces of occupation, but soon it began to grow and gain popularity once again. In 1955 the Japanese Karate Association (JKA) was formed. Two years later, Gichin Funakoshi, who had by now become 'the father of karate', died at the age of 88.

Karate spread to Europe thanks to the efforts of the French martial arts teacher, Henri Plee. Karate went to England through the work and expertise of an unsung innovator, Vernon Bell, who can truly be called the father of English karate.

Modern karate is based upon strikes using punches and kicks combined with many different foot manoeuvres and hip gyrations. Traditionalists, especially from the Okinawan

ABOVE: Dropping his body to achieve maximum leverage, a US soldier throws a comrade over his hip. Though the throw itself could cause damage, follow-up targets would then be the side of the head, the throat or the groin areas.

schools, will not take part in modern karate tournaments and competitions, believing that karate was developed for self-defence, not sport. Shotokan is the most widely followed style. At world level, two governing organisations exist, the World Union of Karate Organisations (WUKO) and the Federation of All-Japan Karate Organisations (FAJKO).

Like kung fu, karate is broken up into many styles, each professing to have within its range of techniques the answer to many combat situations. Karate differs from kung fu, however, in that the movements and applications of the various styles are not very distinct from one another.

As Funakoshi's students became adept at the techniques,

many broke away from the original shotokan school and formed systems of their own. The ones that became major styles in their own right are: shotokan, shotokai, shito-ryu, shukokai, sankukai, wado-ryu, kyokushinkai, goju-ryu, goju-kai and taekwondo (a marriage of Korean traditions with karate). Taekwondo is the most widely practised style, meaning 'way of the foot and fist'. A Buddhist monk, Wong Kwang, originated the five principles that practitioners of taekwondo have adapted as their own – be loyal to your king, be obedient to your parents, be honourable to your friends, never retreat in battle, and kill with justice.

AIKIDO

This art is known as 'the way of harmony' and was created by Morihei Uyeshiba (1883–1969). Uyeshiba had studied classical martial arts as a boy in Japan and went on to develop this relatively recent innovation within the martial arts tradition. Based on avoiding conflict by neutralising an opponent's attacks, it is characterised by flowing, circular movements and the use of 'ki', a mystic vital energy source. Ki is a vital concept within the martial arts. A Japanese term, ki originated from Chinese concepts of chi, which was understood from ancient times as an energy force that dwelt in all living things, though it coalesced in special places and natural phenomena (hills, mist, trees etc.) and also, through the right training, in human beings. Chi is said to flow in certain meridians which run throughout the body – it is these that the acupuncturist attempts to alter with strategically placed needles – and through breathing exercises, martial practice, even sexual control, it was said that chi could be fostered and even directed outwards as a healing, or destructive, force. Chi has been a contentious issue within the martial arts for many years, but it is undoubted that its believers were and are able to demonstrate astounding feats of power beyond their apparent physique. Uyeshiba was one such individual.

Uyeshiba developed the techniques of aikido from his study of the many styles of ju-jitsu in Japan. It is said that the aikido exponent resembles the eye of a hurricane. He remains quiet within himself but he is difficult to overcome because of the circular energy that surrounds him.

LEFT: Swiss Army soldiers at the world-renowned Isone Grenadier School are here utilising leg sweeps to disrupt their opponents' balance – a surprisingly effective and rapid method of gaining combat advantage.

THE TAEKWONDO GENERAL

With its demanding high kicks, taekwondo is not a first choice among military experts in unarmed combat training. In their crowded training schedules, they need techniques that can be taught quickly, without months or years of developing muscle and joint flexibility.

An exception is the Korean military, where crack troops spend long hours kicking ceilings to keep in training. Their exhausting training also includes breaking wood, bricks and concrete slabs with the hands and feet, something which gives the soldiers a tremendous confidence in their ability to deliver decisive blows in combat (a fact which was illustrated by the South Korean soldiers brutal execution techniques during the Vietnam War). South and North Korean forces both have world class competitive and display taekwondo teams.

General Choi Hong Hi was born in northern Korea in 1918. At the age of 12 he began martial arts training in the ancient Korean art of foot fighting, taek kyon. In the 1930s, Choi's pursuit of education took him to Tokyo, where he discovered karate, which became a passion. He was forced to enlist at the outbreak of World War II in 1939. Mostly the war meant prison, however, because he was soon implicated in the Korean independence movement. To keep fit and stave off the boredom, he kept up his karate.

In January 1946 a South Korean army was being formed, and Choi was commissioned as a second lieutenant. A natural leader, he rose quickly, and wherever he was promoted he took his distinctively high-kicking style of karate with him, teaching martial arts to entire companies and regiments under his command, and even to American troops stationed in Korea. By the end of the Korean War in 1953, he was a brigadier general in command of the 5th Infantry Division and the author of a book on military intelligence.

In that year he opened Oh Do Kwan (Gym of My Way) in Seoul. Here he got down to the task of working out exactly what the Choi way was, and with the help of his right-hand man, Nam Tai Hi, formalised into a system the principles and techniques he had been developing out of taek kyon and karate for more than two decades. In 1955 the now Major General Choi christened the system 'taekwondo', helped set up a governing body and embarked energetically on a campaign to take taekwondo, as a sport and self-defence discipline, to the world.

There is a gracefulness in the flowing manner an *aikidoka* moves to avoid an attack – for example, when he takes an attacker's arm and leads him round in a circular movement before grounding him and pinning him with any one of numerous restraints.

Many special forces soldiers favour aikido over other martial arts, because it teaches techniques for fighting several opponents at once, a much more realistic scenario than the one where two sports contestants square up in a controlled situation. Aikido also has specific moves to counter bladed weapons and clubs. This is another area in which the military has built upon aikido to develop unarmed combat techniques.

BRUCE LEE

The 1970s kung fu movies of the legendary Bruce Lee created a new genre in Hollywood. They were immensely successful and are still shown, decades later, around the world. Although fellow martial artists Chuck Norris and Jackie Chan have also had a measure of screen success, Lee stands alone as kung fu's most celebrated celluloid star. He was the most famous student of the wing chun style, which he used as the basis of his own system 'jeet kune do' ('way of the intercepting fist').

Kung fu movies consist mainly of a series of brilliantly choreographed fights accompanied by shrieks and groans, in which one man or woman faces superior numbers, usually armed with knives or clubs, and defeats them by delivering deadly blows with his or her feet and hands. Bruce Lee was a master of that. The plots in his films were always simple good-versus-evil affairs which any spectator could follow. Lee broke box-office records all over the world with his fantasy fighting.

Yet his reputation was based on only four films that he starred in. First he appeared briefly and effectively in *Marlowe* (1969), in which he smashed up James Garner's office. Garner provokes him by remarking: 'You're light on you feet – maybe just a little bit gay?' *Fists of Fury* (also known as The Big Boss), gave Lee his first starring role, then came *The Chinese Connection*, *Return of the Dragon* and *Enter the Dragon*, all with increasing box-office success. *Enter the Dragon* (1973) was Lee's last completed film before his mysterious death at the age of 32.

BEYOND CHINA AND JAPAN

Although China and Japan were central to the development of martial arts over the past 2,000 years, and Korea has had an impact through age-old traditions that contribute to modern taekwondo, many other countries in Asia also developed indigenous fighting systems. Each system, though perhaps not so well known, has produced great masters. The Philippines, for instance, has produced several decidedly lethal forms of unarmed combat. Escrima, or arnis de mano, is one of the most popular. Escrima is an ultra-realistic training in the art of stick fighting, generally using a hardwood stick around 75cm (2.5in) long. Fight training is often brutal in the pursuit of genuinely effective techniques – during some drills blows with the stick are delivered at full power without either party wearing body protection. From the 1950s, the powerful figure of Master Cacoy Canete started to incorporate karate and judo combat moves into the Escrima repertoire to keep the fight going if the stick is lost in combat. Escrima's focus on realism has caught the attention of many in the West, and its techniques have started to filter through into military circles.

Thailand's own powerful martial art, Thai boxing, is a violent unarmed combat system which uses kicks, punches and elbow strikes in full contact training and competitions. In its early days, Thai boxing was extremely dangerous, especially when it was developed into a spectator sport. Before the 1930s, when formal rules and regulations were introduced, contestants would get into a ring wearing crude boxing gloves made of hemp. Often these gloves were dipped in a mixture of glue and ground glass to produce terrifying results. Permanent injury and death were occupational hazards for professional boxers. Almost one in three fights ended in the death of one of the competitors, the most lethal blow being the elbow to the temple, which is now banned.

During the 1970s, Thai boxing was introduced into the United States where it became very popular, partly because it resembles another art introduced at that time, called full-contact karate. Full-contact karate was conceived by a few martial artists tired of the controlled sparring methods allowed in karate and taekwondo. They revolutionised and popularised martial arts when they decided to don boxing gloves and fight in a roped-off ring like professional boxers, so that they could employ full-power kicks and punches against one another instead of having to let their attacks fall just short of a designated target area. Within two years

ABOVE: Combat meets sport. Two kick-boxers exchange blows within the violent yet regulated confines of the ring. The fighter on the left has just delivered a long, high roundhouse kick, which, though spectacular, has left him vulnerable to counter-attack.

television gave them air time and a new spectator sport was born.

Soon after, semi-contact karate came into existence. This allows competitors to fight under virtually the same rules as their full-contact colleagues, but strikes and kicks are judged more on a points system. Points are awarded for perfection of technique rather than for pounding a competitor into the ground or knocking him out.

Thai boxing has also been introduced into Europe, where it has become very popular, with matches and tournaments held on a regular basis. Before long, another form of combat came to the attention of the world's martial arts enthusiasts. It was called kick-boxing and is a combination of muay thai and full-contact karate. Associations were formed and rules instituted. Kick-boxing has gained enormous popularity. Low kicks to the legs are not allowed, but apart from that and a few other rules, kick-boxing is similar to the other martial-art ring-sports.

The full contact forms of martial arts have in the majority of cases severed many of the philosophical links that tie unarmed combat to Eastern spirituality. Yet they have also done unarmed combat training a considerable service. Thai boxing, kick-boxing and full-contact karate have at least removed some of the myths and legends of the invincible martial artist that originated in film and television, and have made trainers much more aware that brute power can usually win over finesse of technique. Yet technique is still important if one is to maximise power and avoid self-inflicted injury, and must be diligently learned by the soldier that means to embark on a rigorous training programme.

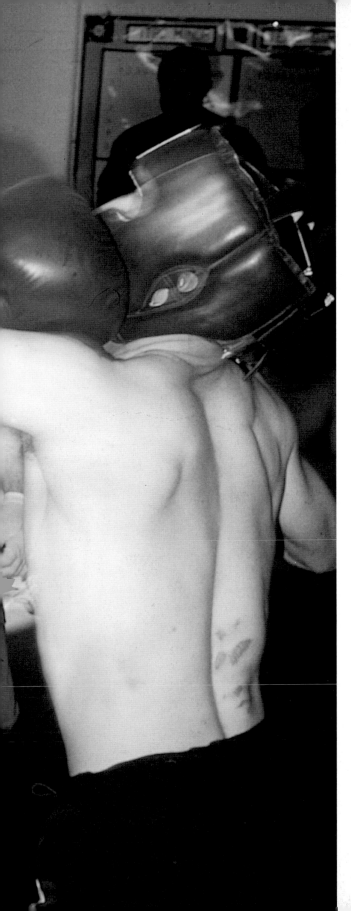

CHAPTER 3

Training Kept Simple

Anyone fighting for his life very quickly reverts to an animal mentality. There may be a period of lucidity for a few seconds and if he is well trained, he will use this automatically to plan his offence.

Military unarmed combat instructors prefer to teach simple techniques with a great deal of emphasis on a few elementary methods which can be easily and instinctively used in combat. The reality is that after a soldier has been hit or stunned by his opponent, he will stop thinking. The blood lust is aroused to the extent that from then on his combat must become instinctive.

To accomplish this simplicity the next step is to make sure that trainees know what target areas of the body to aim for, and which parts of their own bodies to use as weapons, especially the bodily weapons that soldiers can use most naturally. These include the fist, the open hand, the hand drawn into a claw, the knees, the elbows and kicking feet. The soldier is taught how to maximise the damage he can do in hitting, chopping, poking and kicking vital points on the opponent's body with the fist, elbows, knees, feet and the heel and palm of the hand. He is also taught how to stand, how to fall and roll, how to strike and block, how to take an opponent down to ground, and how to choke.

LEFT: **Potential recruits to Britain's Parachute Regiment have to experience 'milling' – when they fight all-out for one minute. Despite the big gloves and headguards, plenty of pain is experienced. The instructor looks on to ensure no fouls are committed.**

41

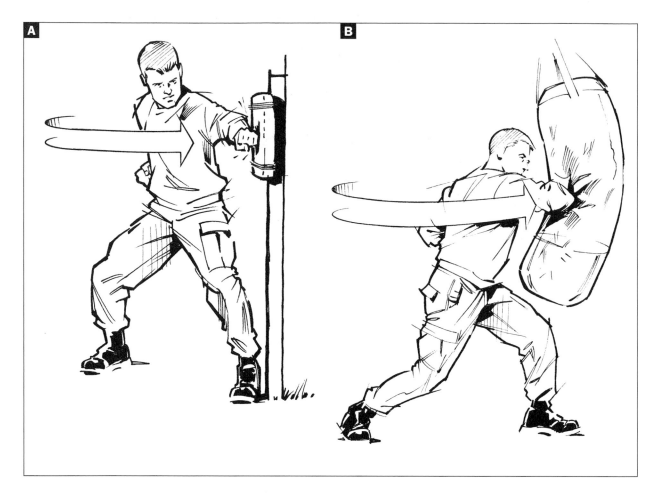

ABOVE: **Two different forms of striking equipment. (A) illustrates the makiwara striking post being used to harden hammer-fist strikes, while (B) shows a soldier applying elbow strikes to a punchbag.**

RIGHT: **A heavy punch bag is ideal for kicking training as its weight will quickly reveal inadequacies in technique. (A) is leaning into a powerful thrust kick while (B) deploys a side thrust kick.**

The techniques taught take into account such possibilities as the soldier's having to fall back on his hands and feet as weapons of last resort in a situation that finds him hungry and near exhaustion. When there is a choice between techniques that require considerable strenuous activity, and others that are quicker, easier and more efficient, even if less artful, the less artful ones will win. In the heat of genuine unarmed combat, economy of movement is essential. Why risk a high kick when a poke in the eye would suffice? There is no need to spend 10 seconds executing a complex set of movements when the same result could be attained with a one-second movement.

Combat without actual weapons in the military is characterised by two guiding principles: brevity and simplicity. At the training stage, selections are made from a vast array of martial arts techniques on offer. Martial arts can teach you how to use just about any part of the human body as a weapon for destroying an opponent. The challenge, however, is to transform a select few of these choices into reliable weapons for the soldier. There are many sources of information on martial arts, but most of them are too complicated and impractical to be useful in the heat of battle.

From his forehead to his toes, the soldier has multiple tools for aggression which, if handled with technique and

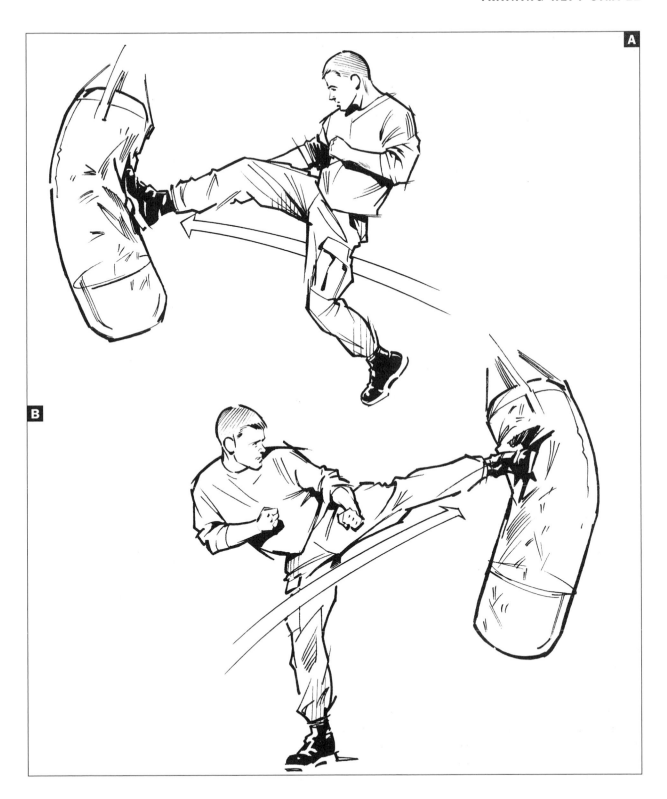

power, can be decisive in an unarmed engagement. Yet today's soldier also needs to have a deep understanding of the potential results of using his natural weapons and must categorise their application accordingly. In incidences of civil disturbance in non-war or peacekeeping zones, elbow strikes to the head would be an inappropriate way to gain a rioter's compliance, as it may kill him or her. Conversely, in an open battlefield situation restraint techniques have little meaning when the opponent is committed to killing you with maximum force. The modern soldier lives in a confusing spectrum of decision across a multiplicity of his roles, and the knowledge which he possesses of unarmed force must be controlled according to circumstances and not just to power.

BELOW: A soldier of the Carabiniers du Prince de Monaco slams a round-house kick into a punchbag steadied by his comrade, conditioning his shins and building up body power.

MAKING THE MOST OF LIMITED TRAINING

Another reason for keeping unarmed combat techniques as simple as possible is that training tends to be limited to a short period. Western elite forces, such as the British Special Air Service (SAS), US Green Berets, US Navy Sea-Air-Land (SEAL) and Belgian Para-Commandos, receive surprisingly little training in the martial arts. Though many members of a unit might be black belts in various martial arts styles, this is more likely because they have pursued martial arts as a personal interest or sport. Often, the techniques incorporated into military training have to be limited enough and flexible enough to be taught in six weeks or less.

Sometimes unarmed combat training is provided for a specific mission. Once the instructor understands the mission of the soldier he is training, the techniques chosen can be tailored for maximum adaptability. Normally, however, the training is aimed at all eventualities. The best

thing to do to prepare for these in a short time is to learn a few tricks that can be taught in a few minutes and used after much practice. One way of accomplishing this is to spare the soldiers from memorising specific techniques but instead teach them to react to general motions – the rounded motion, an overhead strike and so on. For example, the techniques for countering a round punch can also be used against someone using the same motion while swinging a club or pipe.

The unarmed combat techniques chosen usually require no special development of the body, such as significantly improved flexibility. If there is a limited training time, certain physical skills like rolling and falling will improve, but developing the body will not be a prerequisite for the skills to be learned. This means that techniques like high karate kicks are left out.

Martial arts are not an integral part of a special forces soldier's training schedule because there is not enough time to fit it into busy schedules. Higher priority is given to many of the other disciplines required of elite troops, who may need to be proficient in a wide range of skills for

ABOVE: Soviet Airborne Troops stand in ranks and practise the reverse punch, one of the most powerful punching techniques in existence. Note that the back hip is thrust forward as the fist corkscrews at the end of the punch. This directs almost full body weight into the attack.

special operations behind enemy lines and in hostile environments – skills such as demolitions, communications, medicine, survival, combat diving and parachuting. The demands on the time of a special forces soldier are immense, as he is constantly on training courses.

Unarmed combat takes this relatively low priority because even elite troops rarely need to use this skill. They carry reliable small arms. Even training in the use of 'cold' weapons (staffs, knives and bayonets) is less vital than good firearms training. Firearms allow soldiers to fight each other without getting close. Yet the changing face of global military operations from the mid-20th century to the present day has also had a distinct influence on the use and techniques of unarmed combat. Peacekeeping operations now form the most likely scenario for the

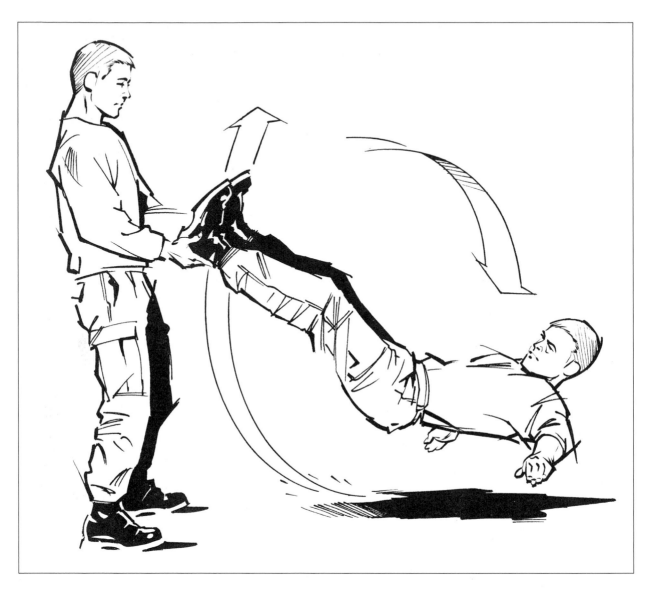

ABOVE: The falling soldier illustrates a classic breakfall technique. By flinging both arms against the ground moments before the body lands, the weight of body impact is reduced, with the result that there is little damage done to the back.

deployment of many armed forces, particularly those from the West. Such duties range from disaster relief in African states to protection of vulnerable communities in the former Yugoslavia. The political and emotional volatility of such operational regions means that soldiers often face aggressive or hostile individuals without the sanction of lethal force. As such, unarmed restraint techniques become vital. In Northern Ireland for example, British soldiers are taught how to put someone rapidly into a headlock or thumb lock (in which the thumb is bent back and pushed up into the armpit) which will cause severe pain to the recipient, but enables the soldier to control the attacker without inflicting physical damage. Recent Australian and Gurkha operations in East Timor required similar capabilities, especially when capturing war crimes suspects. Restraint techniques are thus becoming a much more essential part of military unarmed combat, though as we shall see, actual instruction in these techniques varies considerably.

As we have seen in the case of peacekeeping, however, firepower has its limitations, and unarmed combat should still be an essential part of every soldier's package of skills. Yet the predominant focus on weaponry training means that for most nations the quality and presence of unarmed combat instruction in the military is highly variable. Often it is dependent upon particular units or regiments having their own skilled practitioners who are willing or able to give their time for self-defence courses. Some military forces, however, do have an integral relationship with a particular martial arts programme. We have already noted the association between Korean forces and taekwondo, though South Korean Special Forces also practice the custom-designed combat art of tukong moosul. The Israeli Defence Force has the unique self-defence techniques of Krav Maga as its official unarmed combat programme, most IDF soldiers receiving instruction in its realistic fighting method throughout their period of service. The US Army has a commonly distributed US Army Hand-to-Hand Combat Manual which often forms the basis of each US

soldier's unarmed combat skills. In the former Soviet Union, the elite Spetsnaz troops are all instructed in judo, karate and the home-grown methods of Sambo. In other armies, unarmed combat training is less systematic and is often given in relation to the soldiers' coming operational duties. A British Army soldier destined for Northern Ireland, for instance, or a US soldier deployed in Kosovan peace-keeping, are of necessity taught a fundamental range of restraint and self-defence techniques specific to the likely challenges of crowd disturbance and suspect arrest. Elite counter-terrorist units such the German GSG 9 (Grenzschutzgruppe 9), the French GIGN (Groupement d'Intervention de la Gendarmarie Nationale) and the Taiwanese SWAT are specifically trained in violent suppressive unarmed techniques for use in hostage situations. No overall pattern emerges concerning the way that unarmed combat is instructed throughout the worlds

BELOW: US Army soldiers learn how to defend themselves when grounded and attacked by an upright opponent. The US Army Hand-to-Hand Combat Manual tends to form the basis of training in unarmed combat skills.

ABOVE: Focus pads are great for kicking and punching practice. They are particularly useful for the development of accuracy, power, distancing and multi-angled punches, as anything but a direct hit feels and sounds wrong.

military forces, yet it is certain that those units which neglect such training put themselves at a decisive disadvantage.

BALANCING ACTS

As with other martial arts, one of the basics of military unarmed combat always firmly ingrained in the soldier from the start is keeping his body balanced. The man whose body is not perfectly balanced cannot utilise his strength, and his lack of balance can be used against him. The soldier who attacks most effectively and throws his opponent off-balance has a marked advantage, regardless of difference in size. The use of balance, as well as the use of your opponent's weight and strength against him when he is unbalanced, is one of the basic moves of the ju-jitsu

technique, but even the kind of push or pull that a soldier not highly trained in this art can apply to the shoulders or other parts of the body weakens and breaks an opponent's balance. Once he is off-balance, the opponent's power to initiate an attack is severely weakened.

Keeping your balance mentally, and putting your opponent mentally off-balance, matter as well. To gain the advantage over opponents the soldier will be taught to undermine them physically and undermine them mentally. Anything that can be done to upset the opponent's mental cohesion may be a deciding factor. Shouting, screams, grimaces, growls, groans can be important.

THE BASIC WARRIOR STANCE

A solid stance is critical to good balance and to all other aspects of unarmed combat. The basic warrior stance provides the foundation for all movements and techniques and it is the first thing to be mastered by trainees. It is a matter of keeping the feet the same distance apart as the width of the shoulders, like a boxer's stance. To ensure the best balance, the feet should never be stretched wide apart or placed close together. Like a stylish boxer, the soldier trained in unarmed combat keeps his knees slightly bent and arms low.

It is very much like a boxer's stance; so if you are unsure what it looks like, simply study two boxers squaring up to each other. To feel for yourself what the basic warrior stance is like:

- Place your feet shoulder-width apart with the toe of the rear foot in line with the heel of the front foot. Feet should point 45 degrees from the direction of the attack.
- Bend slightly at the knees, making sure your body weight is evenly distributed on both legs.
- Bend your elbows to form 45 degree angles.
- Hold your arms high enough to protect your face without blocking your vision.
- Keep your elbows close to your body to protect your ribs.
- Curl your fingers into a fist but do not clench your fists – clenching contracts the forearm muscles and detracts from hand speed and reaction time.
- Tuck your chin down to take advantage of the natural protection provided by your shoulders.

In hand-to-hand fighting a well-trained soldier can assume the basic warrior stance instinctively and move in all directions while maintaining it. During movement, his legs or feet do not cross and his upper body remains in the basic warrior stance. The knees bend deeper than normal. Movement is executed through his legs moving in a shuffling motion so that they remain equidistant, making it easier to maintain balance. It is best practice not to bend from the waist. If possible, the soldier uses hand movements by way of feints and strikes to conceal the movement of legs and feet.

Forward movement is achieved by sliding the lead foot forward half a pace. As soon as the lead foot is in place, the rear foot moves forward quickly to return to the basic warrior stance. To move backward, the soldier does the forward movement in reverse. Again, a boxer's movement around the ring are a good model for the trainee.

To change direction, the technique is to turn the head quickly to the new direction, push off with lead leg and quickly step in the new direction while pivoting on the ball of the rear foot.

PRACTISE MAKES PERFECT

Practical learning of unarmed combat tactics ensures that a soldier can assess conditions and situations and instinctively select the most effective. But any hand-to-hand combat training that uses set positions for the attacker and his opponent is useless in real-life situations. The only solution for soldiers preparing for genuine life-or-death fighting is to hone skills through many hours of practising their reactions to attacks. Constant practise on dummies and on bags and equipment is also a prerequisite for getting battle fit.

GENERATING PHYSICAL POWER

The two central tenets of physical power in unarmed combat are relaxation and total body commitment to the blow. Relaxation and physical looseness often surprise new recruits to unarmed combat training, generally because a tensed muscle is associated with strength. However, a tense muscle is a slow muscle, and blows have to be delivered with speed otherwise they can simply become forceful pushes rather than debilitating strikes. Any successful unarmed combat technique should use a mixture of relaxation and tension. In the case of a punch, for instance, the arm should be kept as loose as possible prior to actual contact with the target, thus allowing the fist to whip out with speed. Tension is, however, required upon actual contact, locking every muscle in the body to provide a solid base for the transference of energy from the punch into the target. This locking of the body in turn indicates the essential principle of total body commitment. A nine-stone man fighting a taller 14-stone man is at an undoubted disadvantage in a fight, yet if the smaller man can transfer his nine stone of weight through every kick and strike then the contest is very much more equal. Using the split-second locking of the body on impact and an absolute commitment of his whole frame to any blow, any soldier can generate enormous destructive impact. Particularly vital is control of the waist and the shoulders, as these points, if not properly solid, can twist on impact and retract some of the force of a punch or kick. The moment of contact can be accompanied by a violent scream or shout (known in the martial arts as a kiai). This is not just for intimidation – shouting forces air from the body and this greatly increases muscle tension in the chest and abdomen for more solid attacks.

ABOVE: Egyptian rangers stand in the baking heat and practise a classic karate rising block aimed at deflecting a punch above the head. Note that the non-blocking hand is withdrawn to the waist; this imparts body twist to the technique, which in turn puts more weight behind the block.

As with all physical training that is conscious of health and safety, the practise sessions start with warm-up exercises and stretches to get muscles ready for the stresses and strains they are about to undergo. Warm-ups include bending, squatting and push-ups. As a rule they are done after short runs. Repetitions vary in number from five to ten.

The training drill will probably be divided into various stages, each involving ample repetition. The first stage, typically, is one of practising in pairs or groups, with one or more men attacking, one man defending. Most soldiers will already have some experience in fighting, maybe from competitive wrestling or merely from schoolyard fighting as kids, and at this stage, they are largely practising what they already know. Practise takes place in an area that provides room for ground fighting and close contact, but which is free of obstacles that could cause injuries. A sand pit is excellent for this. The following drills are the ones msot likely to be used.

Two-man combat. Two soldiers enter the combat area and fight each other for a specific period, say, one 30-second round. There are no rules or objectives, just freestyle fighting.

Tag-team continuous. The soldiers are paired off and one man from each pair enters the pit and fights another soldier until he is tired. Then, when he can find an opening, he tags in his partner. The fight goes on for several minutes. Again, there are no rules and no objectives.

Wave attack. One soldier stands in the centre of the sand pit and has the others surround him. One at a time each soldier attacks him and fights him until told to change. Each soldier stays in the middle until he has fought all the others.

Combat alley. A soldier walks through an area filled with obstacles, between which a few other soldiers are hiding, waiting to attack. The soldier fights against random, spontaneous attacks by the other soldiers.

Blind battle. Much of the work the soldier does takes place at night. A good way to simulate darkness is to use a simple blindfold. Each soldier is attacked while he is blindfolded in any of the scenarios already described. The soldiers also practise at night.

The main tendency that will appear during stage-one training is that the soldiers perceive the fight to start when they are making physical contact. In the next stage, which begins after a few days of this relatively aimless fighting, they will therefore need to learn to see the openings that present themselves when someone is moving from intermediate to grappling range. And instead of finding an entry point from which to take their opponent to the ground, they will be taught disabling techniques that allow them to stay, themselves, on their feet.

What these stage-one practise routines often make plain is that untrained soldiers rarely know how to end a fight other than some sort of simple submission, or perhaps just physical exhaustion. When they move on to stage two, instructors will ensure that any defence or attack action practised is taken to its logical end, with each man trying to stop, pin, disarm, tie up or capture his partner.

SPECIFIC TRAINING

During stage-two training, the soldier learns what the objective of hand-to-hand fighting is – to survive. This may seem like stating the obvious, but it is always worth bringing home to trainees that any time an unarmed encounter enters the range of grappling, the enemy's sole purpose will be to disable or kill him; and so the soldier must make it his own objective to disable or kill, and get away.

During stage two, the soldiers are taught to improve their responses to openings and to find ways of finishing a fight quickly. They learn the possible weak points that may present themselves before contact is made, as well as those that present themselves after combat has entered a grappling or a ground-fighting phase.

They might be taught that when the opponent has lowered himself into a wrestler's crouch and is rushing in, they can counter-attack with eye gouges, cupping the ears, knees to the face and elbows to the back of the head, spine and base of the skull. They can follow through with the techniques necessary to finish the attacker completely.

If the attacker and the soldier are already making physical contact, they will learn that strategy remains the same: they should try to use disabling techniques. Nose smashes, eye gouges, strikes to the throat and the neck and a whole range of other such devastating techniques can end a fight fast. They must learn what the possibilities are and then learn to exploit them.

Another possibility when rolling around on the ground is a favourite of blockbuster movies – the weapon of opportunity. Finding a rock and hitting an opponent in the head or throwing sand in his eyes can turn the tide of a personal battle dramatically.

Here are some drills commonly used for stage-two training. One weapon, one target. One target and one weapon are chosen and one technique constantly drilled. For example, going for one eye with one hand and gouging it when someone rushes at you in a crouched posture.

Avoidance and evasion. This exercise teaches soldiers how to avoid, evade and outmanoeuvre an opponent's attack. For example, one soldier attacks another using a single technique. During the first stage of the drill, the defending soldier evades his opponent's attack using only body movement. During the second stage of the drill, the defending soldier evades his opponent's attack and then follows with a counter-attack. The techniques used to evade the attacks are similar to those practised in aikido and ju-jitsu.

Grounded. This drill should be started with one soldier dominating another soldier on the ground by sitting on his

THE MAKIWARA

A common piece of training equipment amongst Far Eastern forces, the makiwara has featured in martial arts instruction since ancient times. Its basic construction consists of a solid oak plank or post standing to chest height and securely set in the ground. The top of the post is usually wrapped with cord. This is the striking surface, and in training it is punched or kicked to condition the limbs for combat and also develop the power and speed of attacking techniques. An essential value of the makiwara is that it teaches the student to attack with force and yet retract his fist or leg at speed before the whiplash of the post can do him any damage. This is useful training as it teaches the soldier not to leave a limb outstretched which could be grabbed or damaged by his opponent.

chest or sticking a knee in his back. An actual fight never starts this way, of course, but this drill requires good combinations of strength and technique to prevail. The soldiers learn for themselves what is most effective and what doesn't work.

The general pattern for stage two is that the trainees practise specific defensive moves and attacks with blows, kicks and, once an opponent loses his balance or attention, throws. They also learn how to use retreating, bending, twisting and repelling moves in attack and defence, as well as employing physical objects as weapons of opportunity.

The soldiers continue to fight each other repeatedly to discover their strengths and weaknesses. Stances are practised, as are masking moves and psychological devices such as using feints to get the opponent to make a make a mistake. The soldiers also practise foul blows, hand and arm defences.

The soldiers will be taught how to use their weight, momentum, speed and reflexes in attack and defence. They

learn how to complete a manoeuvre after being forced onto the defensive and they get first-hand experience in how the tempo of unarmed combat is affected by extra burdens such as flak jackets, personal equipment, heavy boots or snow.

The difference in teaching these techniques to soldiers as compared to a traditional martial arts student rests mainly in the time spent learning nuances. A soldier doesn't have the luxury of time at the training stage, and in the heat of battle he doesn't have the luxury of nuance; so the choices will be limited. Effective response equals narrowness of options and enhanced skill in their use.

THE FINAL STAGE OF TRAINING

During a final stage of training, soldiers normally return to the drills and exercises from their first days but apply the techniques, strategies and tactics learned in stage two. The key now is the repetition of a narrow range of responses and their fluid application in natural fight-like encounters. They try to avoid the use of sheer strength and work harder on the application of technique. Once the techniques are learned, both speed and power can be increased.

Finally, they learn unarmed combat under increasingly difficult conditions, such as freeing themselves from an enemy's hold in the midst of a chaotic situation. They learn how, in an unexpected encounter with the enemy, they might attack effectively using one or a combination of the methods they have been practising.

At all stages, learning the technical side of unarmed combat will go hand in hand with building up physical strength and agility and psychological conditioning.

QUICK-FIX TRAINING

If a soldier has only six weeks unarmed combat training, the first week or so may be devoted to highly focused counter-attack drills. One method is to have trainees face each other and then alternate counter-attacking each other using a single technique such as a claw to the face – nothing more. They may move in circles, manoeuvre around obstacles, or roll around on the ground, but the only technique they can use is a claw to the face until it seems completely obvious and natural. Then they repeat

LEFT: The focus pads are also ideal for knee kick practice. The attacker delivers maximum power by swinging his knee hard in an upward arc while pulling down on his partner's collar for extra compressive force.

FIGHTING IN UNIFORM

All soldiers must learn to apply unarmed combat techniques while dressed in full uniform rather than PT kit or light fatigues. In a typical Combat Order dress, the soldier will typically be carrying a basic webbing system and weaponry which even without a backpack could be many kilograms in weight. This weight around the waist and shoulders can severely restrict movement in an unarmed combat situation, especially if heavy straps have also reduced blood flow to the arms. Furthermore, cold weather clothing can hamper punching and kicking speed because of bulky material around the armpits, elbows and knees. In such cases, grappling techniques can be more appropriate and the extra weight of webbing can be used to deliver more momentum in a grappling clash. Boots are also a major consideration in unarmed combat techniques. If the soldier has only trained in light training shoes, knee dislocation could result when he kicks for the first time with his boots on owing to the extra momentum generated by the boot weight. In all cases, unarmed combat instruction must train the recruits at some point in the gear and clothing in which they may have to fight. More uniform and load-carrying designs are starting to pay heed to the soldiers need for physical manoeuvrability. Modern chest webbing systems, such as the advanced US PASGT system (Personal Armour System Ground Troops), allow the soldier to carry his equipment in a close-fitting vest-style jacket which not only allows free movement of the arms but also keeps equipment closer to the soldier's centre of gravity and thus reduces the risk of imbalance during a close-quarters fight.

this exercise using other techniques, such as elbows or knees to the body.

Arguably the best form of unarmed combat counter-attacking derives from the kajukenbo style of martial arts training. The soldier is taught to block or parry and at the same time launch the first counter-attack technique, trying to prevent the attacker from reacting by stunning or disabling him. Then the soldier moves directly to a takedown, finishing the attacker on the ground.

Each technique is actually a series that becomes a reflex. When the time comes to train the soldiers in

counter-attacking, they are not given a free choice of how to respond until the last two weeks of training. The rest of the course is spent developing a few simple counter-attack combinations until the soldier can flow through each set without hesitation.

The secret is to keep the options to a minimum, which includes the number of combinations to be taught. For example, a soldier might be taught just:

- ten combinations against empty-hand attacks,
- five against kicks,
- ten against several common grab, pulling or pushing situations,
- five against knives,
- two against guns.

All follow the same basic strategy of parry, stun, take-down and finish.

One key for making unarmed combat work effectively is to instil in the soldier that once he launches his counter-attack, he does not stop until the attacker is finished. When the soldier has his attacker on the ground, he is required to continue with at least four techniques, such as kicks to the head or ribs, chokehold or strike to the neck or throat.

During the last two weeks of training, the fighting situations may consist of a series of unannounced and unpredictable situations where all a soldier can do is to react, such as walking through a course set with traps. Through the informal, crudely constructed course where others are waiting behind obstacles to attack him, he learns from reacting in ambush scenarios. A variation is to send two soldiers through the hidden attack course together.

These methods are specifically designed for soldiers who will be using the training in a combat environment where taking prisoners is not a priority.

EQUIPMENT

Focus pads are essential for training and are common in all martial arts and boxing gyms. They are excellent for the development of accuracy, power, distancing and multi-angled punches. Each pad is centred by a target spot and anything but a direct hit on the spot looks, feels and

LEFT: A Marine Corps soldier is catapulted into the air by a hip throw. Even as he falls, his left arm is extending to execute a break fall, and on landing he may be able to retaliate with kicks to his attacker's groin, shins or knees.

BELOW: A stretch for the back muscles. This position is often held for some time and is surprisingly comfortable, a factor which makes the muscles relax and stretch even more. These exercises should be used at the end of each training session.

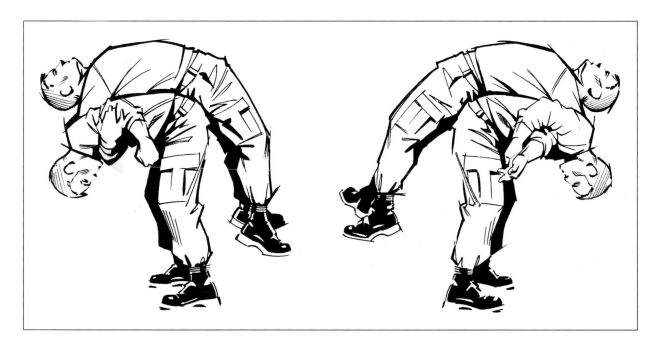

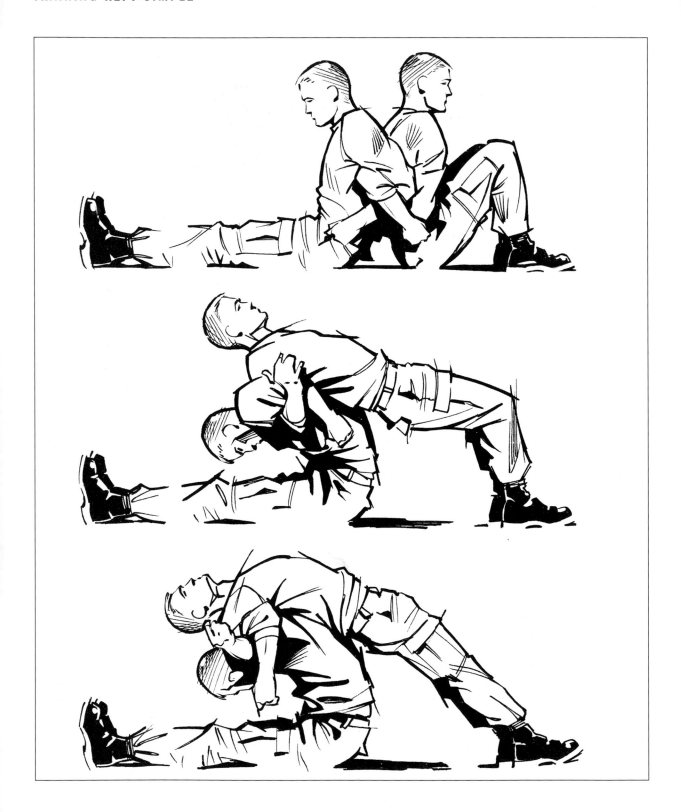

LEFT: **A similar stretch to that shown on page 55, but here delivered from a sitting position. As the soldier on the left pulls forward, his partner on the right pushes forward from a bent-leg position and stretches his back. Care must be taken not to over-extend the spine.**

ABOVE: **A dynamic tension stretch in which the side chest muscles are stretched by locking hands with a partner to the side and pulling, while keeping the chest presented to the front. As well as stretching the muscles, this exercise builds upper-body strength.**

sounds wrong. An accurate shot will feel solid and emit a definite 'thwack', letting the soldier know that he is on target. They are excellent for anyone wishing to develop a knockout punch.

It is necessary to work in pairs when practising with the pads. One fits one pad to each hand and then angles them to meet the demand of a desired punch from the other. He faces the spot on the pads inward for hook punches, downward for uppercuts and forward for straight punches. The soldier punching employs a guard in normal practice and no guard in 'line-up' practice. The holder varies the height and distance of the pads from the puncher.

As the puncher hits the pads he exhales through his mouth or nose. This regulates the breathing, feeds the working muscles with oxygen and aids body focus, forcing the muscles to tense on impact of the punch or strike.

Once the puncher becomes familiar with hitting the pads, the holder may dictate and control the play by shouting out strikes for the puncher to execute. 'Double jab, right cross and left hook,' for instance. He changes the angle of the pads to receive the designated strikes. The experienced puncher may attempt more advanced combinations. The holder does not stay in the same position all the time. He moves, forcing the puncher to employ footwork. Each time the puncher finishes his punch or combination, the holder moves to a different position.

Focus pads are good for practising front snap kicks – using the instep rather than the ball of the foot – and roundhouse kicks. They help to develop power, distancing and accuracy. A pad held to the thigh may be used to practise low roundhouse kicks. If tucked under the opposite armpit, target area pointing outward, it is ideal for midsection roundhouse kicks. If held at groin level, with the target area pointing to the floor, it may be used to practise

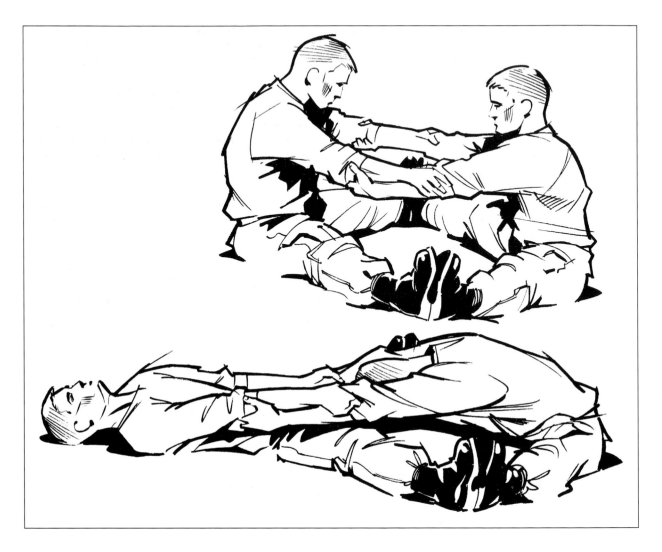

ABOVE: The soldier on the right here undergoes a groin-stretching exercise. His legs are held wide open by his partner and his torso is then drawn very slowly forward to reach maximum strength.

low front snap kicks, using the instep of the foot to attack. If held across and slightly in front of the body, target area pointing outward and at head height, it may be used for head-level roundhouse kicks.

Focus pads are not as effective as the heavy bag for practising knee attacks, but still quite good. The holder holds one pad tightly against his thigh with the target area pointing outward while the attacker thrusts his knee roundhouse-fashion into the pad. To practise the upward knee strike, the holder puts both padded hands in front of

himself at about groin height, right hand overlapping left with both palms facing toward the floor. The attacker may take hold of the holder's hands and pull them downward into the uprising knee or alternatively, grab his clothing at shoulder level and pull on them as he executes the knee attack on the pads.

Life-size dummies, complete with arms, head and legs, are essential in training for unarmed combat. The vital spots are marked on the dummies and the trainees are made to practise daily with no restraint on all hand and foot blows they have learned. Five or six dummies might be suspended in a confined space, like in a boxing ring. One trainee at a time enters the ring and as fast as he can attacks the dummies at random, using every kind of blow with hand, foot, knee, elbow and head, from any position.

Suspended in mid-air on a length of elastic from floor to ceiling, the top and bottom ball serves as a wonderful piece of equipment for the development of timing and distancing. It is considered the closest soldiers in training can get to a real opponent. It is also an enjoyable method of practice. It may be used to practise jabs, crosses, hooks and uppercuts. The height and thus the speed of the ball can easily be altered by tightening the straps above and below the ball. In practice, if the trainee stands close to the ball he has to be vigilant to avoid being hit back on its return. This adds to the realism of the practice immeasurably.

The punch bag is probably the oldest method of practice known to the fighting man. Despite its ancient heritage, it is still the very best power-developing implement on the market. It is excellent for developing good technique, stamina and combination punching. Because of the punch bag's mass, it does not help in developing accuracy, but it helps everything else.

Punch bags are ideal for practising front kicks, roundhouse kicks, side kicks and back kicks. If the bag is placed flat on the floor it is also a very good tool for practising stamping kicks.

When trainees are executing front kicks, side kicks and back kicks on the punch bag, it can be swung and kicked as it moves back and forth. This is excellent for practising distancing on a moving target. For low kicks and sweeps, a long 2m (6-foot-6-inch) bag that hovers just above the ground is recommended.

The best way to practise knee attacks on the punch bag is to 'clothe it' by tying a loose sack around it or dressing it in old clothes, so that the trainee can grip, grab and knee it like he would a real opponent. Again, the bag can

BELOW: **A strong set of stomach muscles is vital if the unarmed combatant is to withstand body punches and deliver strong attacks. The exercise pictured here enables two soldiers to practice sit-ups while competitively matching the demands of the other's endurance.**

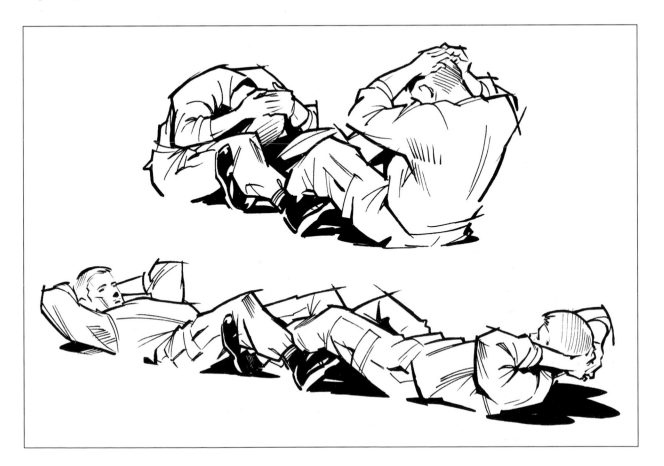

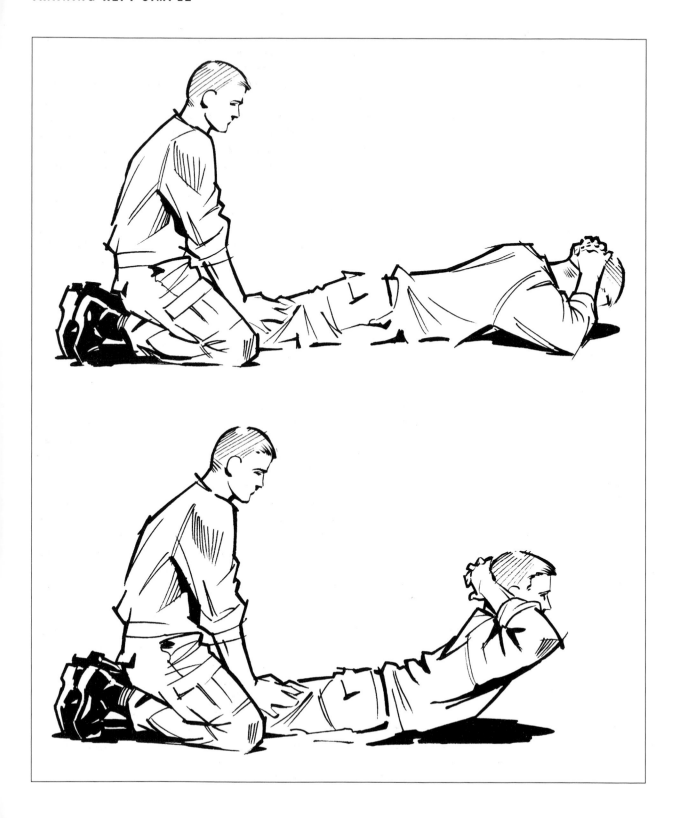

be swung. Down on the floor, it can be used for knee-drop practice. A 2m bag is great for practising lower region strikes.

Set at a height just above a person's own head, the speed ball is good for building the deltoid (shoulder) muscles and quickening hand-to-eye coordination, which is why it is an integral part of boxers' training.

The greatest form of practice, without doubt, is to be had with a training partner or opponent with whom soldiers can communicate, learn and progress. Tell each other when a technique feels right, wrong, realistic, unrealistic, powerful or weak and so on. If a soldier does not, or cannot train with a partner, that person should make bag or pad work as realistic as possible by using visualisation. Imagine that training equipment is the real antagonist and this is a real situation. Try to charge every blow with aggression, perhaps imagining that a life depends on the success or failure of the strike.

REALISM IN MILITARY TRAINING

Injecting realism into unarmed combat training is an essential part of any military instruction programme if the techniques learned are to have some practical value. Many seasoned martial artists have had the demoralising experience of becoming expert in the dojo and competition hall, but find themselves easily overcome by an untrained opponent in the more scrappy, less predictable environment of actual combat. Realistic training thus enables the soldier to experience what works and what doesn't and also adjust mentally to the shock of pain and aggression. There are several essential principles of combat realism. The first is to impose an element of actual danger. SAS soldiers training in knife defence, for example, will work from doing the drills with a rubber knife to actually using a live blade; the confidence gained from handling the real thing means a less nervous response to actual knife attack. The second principle is to train in the clothes in which you will fight, as uniform and equipment can severely restrict the physical weapons available to any soldier in combat. Thirdly, unpredictability is vital to introduce later in the instruction programme. Again the SAS in its Close-Quarters Battle (CBQ) training achieves this by forcing each soldier through

LEFT: While much attention is paid to building up strong stomach muscles, less is given to the equally vital lower back muscles (which can give some protection to the kidneys if developed). This exercise uses small movements repeated many times to develop muscle tone.

series of combat-response exercises in various urban, vehicular and outdoor locations without informing them of the opponents arraigned against them. The CBQ programme also illustrates the principle of training in the environments in which you will fight. Long, high kicks, for instance, are useless in many building environments where tables, chairs and other objects restrict movement. Thus elite anti-terrorist units such as the French GIGN and the Spanish GEO train inside mock-up buildings and aircraft interiors to ensure that their operatives know the limits of their unarmed options in any fighting location. Finally, it is useful for soldiers to gain some experience of delivering their techniques with full power. Spetsnaz soldiers often wear body armour during unarmed combat training so that kicks and punches to the torso can be delivered with total commitment. This is invaluable to know whether one is developing enough physical strength to win through in an actual fight. If all these ingredients are introduced into a military training programme, then the soldier will be able to go into combat knowing he has fully prepared for the eventualities of combat and that he has techniques which if used will achieve what he intends.

FITNESS AND UNARMED COMBAT

Any unarmed fight is acutely exhausting. The combination of mental tension, powerful and abrupt physical exhaustion and the effort of coping with pain can drain away a combatant's martial potency in seconds if he does not have a good foundation of physical fitness. Fitness training for unarmed combat should mix both aerobic and anaerobic methods. Aerobic exercises, which focus on increasing cardiovascular efficiency in transporting and absorbing oxygen around the body, include running, circuits and swimming and are essential to building up the combatant's overall endurance. Anaerobic exercises, these being exercises which focus on muscle performance (and not on cardiovascular maximisation), provide the requisite stamina for rapid muscle movements, and include weight training and martial arts training itself. Mixing the aerobic and anaerobic exercises is essential to provide the all-round physical qualities demanded in unarmed combat. Good fitness can be the linchpin in a fight, as it helps the soldier control breathing and also resist the limb fatigue that will weaken his techniques. Fortunately, the rigorous physical training programmes maintained in most military units provides the soldier with this all-round physical competence.

Mental Training

The primary weapon a soldier has to develop to be proficient in unarmed combat is his mind. His ability to think and react under pressure without panicking is vital.

As with any other martial art, one of the primary reasons for training soldiers in unarmed combat is to give them a decided mental edge. Like a boxer preparing for a fight, if a soldier has trained for unarmed combat he will have the psychological advantage over an untrained opponent. The boxer believes that if he has trained really hard and is mentally 'up' for a contest, his opponent will not beat him – so too a soldier well prepared in unarmed combat. The techniques themselves may not even be used, but it is invaluable insurance in a soldier's mind if he has plenty of unarmed combat training to call upon.

The soldier needs to develop his mind. He has to be able to react without panicking and in a split second. A good soldier continually trains with this goal in mind. He needs to hone his ability to keep his head in a violent empty-hands fighting encounter.

The principles of unarmed combat are largely those of judo and various other styles of wrestling, boxing, kick-boxing and self-defence. The importance of this type of combat lies not only in the extreme offensive skill which the exponent can achieve, but also in the fact that any man, regardless of size or physique, once well trained in this technique, has a supreme confidence in himself and his fighting abilities which he could not achieve in any other way.

LEFT: These trainees are being put through an intense training programme that seeks to make them believe in their own ability – a good soldier must be mentally strong as well as physically prepared – an altogether tougher form of training.

ABOVE: Japanese Samurai warriors – the Japanese were well known for their mental strength in battle. The age of the warrior for the Japanese began long ago with the Samurai who were fearless warriors.

RESPECT FOR DANGER

Nevertheless, a well-trained soldier never assumes that he is against an untrained adversary. By making such an assumption falsely he may lay himself open to an unexpectedly expert attack. When a soldier puts himself in position to apply encumbering holds, he is also putting himself in a position where an enemy can counter-attack with hand or foot blows.

Confidence is a great attribute, but over-confidence is a very weak link. It leads to defeat. Special forces soldiers are trained to watch out for their own over-confidence, to remind themselves of the possible dangers they are facing and of the consequences of defeat.

They are taught to be basic, never employing a technique for the sake of dramatic effect. Looking good counts for nothing. All that matters is to find the quickest, most economical solution to the problem at hand. That means being quick. A well-trained soldier doesn't hang around. If he is going to attack the enemy he does so as quickly as possible, especially when dealing with more than one adversary. Any time delay in making a pre-emptive attack will lessen his chances of success.

Nevertheless if a soldier can retreat from a situation or talk his way out of a fight, his training tells him he should. Survival is all that matters. Pride has no place in unarmed combat in the military.

MASTERING FEAR

Fear control is very important. This is another of the foundations on which self-confidence is built. When danger arises and adrenaline spills into the bloodstream, it is there to speed our fight against the danger or power our flight away from it. You have to chose whether it will be fight or flight, and if you postpone making this choice until the danger arises – when calm deliberation is not available – the wrong choice is easily made. The shock factor of adrenaline can be frightening if you do not understand or expect it. It can make a soldier freeze in the face of an attack.

A fundamental of all military training is to make 'fight' the impulsive choice. For no one is this more important than the soldier fighting hand to hand. Flight will only bring pursuit, and the advantage (the opportunities to maim or kill) will all be on the side of the pursuer. Hesitation – while considering whether to fight or flee – will simply hand that advantage to him through your own loss of the initiative. Indecision can spell defeat. Even a split second lost can mean the difference between life and death, survival and destruction.

Cus D'Amato, Mike Tyson's late trainer always said: 'Fear is the friend of exceptional people.' He meant the surge of adrenaline that brings fear is the same surge of adrenaline that makes it possible to fight. But your mental conditioning must be up to it. If a soldier's body is a gun, his hands and feet the bullets, then his mind is the trigger. Absence of the trigger renders the rest of the gun ineffective. Physically well-conditioned bag punchers and mirror watchers, convinced in their own minds that they can 'handle themselves', may fold up in a really threatening situation. However, with a properly conditioned mind – a tough mind – a soldier confronting danger moves safely through the adrenaline build-up, the stress and pain of a physical encounter.

He does not panic, but harnesses the feeling, fine tuning it into a laser line of ferocious aggression that can be turned on and off with pin-point accuracy, channelled with devastating results onto his enemy. In a fear-inspiring

BELOW: US Marine Security Guard trainees use non-lethal repellant to disarm or repel an assailant by squirting them into their eyes. The effect is instantaneous and painful. Part of a soldier's mental training is to realise that a successful defence is often the simplest.

situation, a soldier's legs may start to shake, his mouth become dry and pasty and his voice may even acquire a nervous quiver. His training teaches him to ignore these feelings – they are all part and parcel of the adrenaline build-up, and though unpleasant, quite natural; and they tend to lessen in intensity as he becomes more exposed to them. Fear that has been mastered becomes a fast-moving vehicle with the soldier at the steering wheel.

TOUGH MINDEDNESS

Soldiers who are being trained in unarmed combat are taught to be hard, not to allow sentiment to enter their minds when dealing with the enemy. A trained soldier must never forget that the enemy is out to kill him.

BELOW: British Army recruits use various methods of training to improve the mental as well as the physical aspect of their skills – a soldier also needs to learn how to deal with pain. Fitness and aggression are vital elements of any soldier's character.

The soldier can't afford to be squeamish. If sticking fingers in an adversary's eyes or squeezing his testicles is the only option to survive, he will do it. So he forgets fair play. When a soldier is under threat of attack, there is no such thing as fair play. He does anything and uses anything to defend himself. There is only one rule – there are none.

He also learns not to be suckered, to be very sceptical of an enemy who is offering to shake hands or plea bargain. It is very often a ploy to dupe a soldier into letting down his guard. If he accepts such an offer, a trained soldier does so warily; it is preferable not to find oneself in this situation. The same ploy is often worked by someone offering a cigarette and then striking out as the person receives it. The London East End gangster Reggie Kray was famous for his 'cigarette punch'. He would offer an adversary a cigarette and then punch him on the jaw as he was about to light it knowing full well that the jaw would be relaxed and easily broken.

BEYOND PAIN

To be successful in unarmed combat against weapons, a soldier must learn how to function with pain, ignoring it for the moment in order to respond effectively in the face of great danger. It's either that or suffer even greater pain – and perhaps death – at the hands of the attacker.

Learning to overcome pain is one of the greatest and most important challenges a soldier has to face. He will have suffered much physical pain in the hard weeks of training. It is never easy. Reactions to pain vary not only from person to person, but for the same person under different circumstances, but with determination, anyone can learn to achieve an adequate degree of control over his response to pain. There are many stories of soldiers who have suffered broken bones or taken other severe injuries in the heat of battle and still finished the fight on top. They are not superhuman fighters, just fighters who believe they can carry on; and so they do.

Though pain control is important in unarmed combat, it's still critical that a soldier should listen to his body. Pain is often an indicator that something is seriously wrong. During defence against an armed opponent, it's crucial that a soldier should push himself beyond the pain, but it's equally important that he not hurt himself while training. That would be dangerous and self-defeating.

VISUALISING SUCCESS

When a soldier is learning unarmed combat, as when he is learning many other military skills, he faces a fundamental paradox: how does he practise and master beforehand something whose actual application may result in the opponent's death? The answer has two parts. The soldier first must learn the actual physical skills involved, such as kicking, evasive movement and the like. The second part relies on visualisation, whether this be undertaken in a structured way as part of his training, or whether it is something that he just does anyway.

Professional and amateur sportsmen, especially in recent years, have learned to depend more on consciously developing a complex set of natural mental skills, which include visualising the performance, performance emotions and perfection of technique. The soldier can adopt the same training methods and adapt them to his own ends.

Soldiers appreciate two aspects of any kind of training: that it is pragmatic and practical and that its results are clearly apparent. There are ways to train soldiers so that they witness the benefits of mental training without

ABOVE: Yogi Vithaldas in the Padma-Asan (Lotus pose), one of the meditative postures. Though the martial arts and Eastern religions have long used meditation and visualisation, it still remains on the periphery of military training, usually for the most elite recruits.

having to wait a lifetime, especially when the reasons for and results of training are put into terms directly applicable to them.

SIMPLE RELAXATION

A soldier should take a comfortable position, such as lying on his back or sitting cross-legged. Once comfortable, he runs a mental inventory of himself. Starting at the top of his head and working down his body to his toes, he tightens and then relaxes each body part in turn while taking deep breaths. For example, he takes a deep breath as he squints his eyes, then lets the air out slowly as he relaxes the muscles around the eyes.

THE IMPORTANCE OF VISUALISATION

Top sportsmen are unanimous in their praise for visualisation and are even prepared to be hypnotised to attain it.

ABOVE: US Marines who are part of the Marine Security Guard School train at Marine Corps Base, Quantico, Virginia. Stamina training is just as important as learning fighting techniques.

Visualisation is used with great success by doctors and psychologists. Yet it still lies under a shadow of disbelief and ignorance. Sceptics scoff at the very thought of programming the mind through visualisation, but there is a lot of positive documentation on the topic.

Visualisation is a multi-tiered phenomenon in that it can be used to attain many things, from building confidence to perfecting technique to confronting fears. In a recent visualisation experiment in America, two groups of students were asked to practise basketball penalty shots everyday for a month. One group physically practised netting the ball while the other group lay on a bed or sat in a chair and using visualisation, mentally practised netting the ball.

At the end of the month both groups met at a basketball court and competed to see which of the two could net the most shots. The group that had practised using visualisation won by a considerable margin.

The value of visualisation is that it gives the brain a model for events and techniques it has not yet experienced or accomplished. As human beings we are able to perform common tasks, such as making a meal, driving a car etc., because they have been repeated enough times for the brain to make a model of how they are done and the body actions that accompany their performance. Yet we frequently come up against tasks and demands with which we are not familiar. In such circumstances, the brain searches for the closest matching model and attempts to adapt it to the task in hand with varying levels of success.

Yet ironically the brain cannot tell the difference between a model based on direct experience and a model based on imagined experience. Consequently, visualisation enables the brain to build up a model of an unfamiliar experience prior to actually encountering that experience in the real world. The secret to its application is to build up as vivid a mental image as possible. If a soldier wants to train himself to respond appropriately in an unarmed fight, he must not only picture in his mind's eye the techniques he would use, but he must also imagine such details as colours, noises, expressions, the sensations within his own body, pain and anything else which adds realism to the visualisation. The repetition of this exercise gathers into a mental model for dealing with actual unarmed combat situations and though the image may not be a perfect match to the real world, if pictured vividly enough it can precondition the soldier to the stress of real physical combat.

That isn't to say that a soldier should replace physical practice with visualisation, but certainly use it as a strong supplement. In a combat sense the use of visualisation is useful. People who believe in it claim anything is attainable through its conscientious practice.

Many top martial arts competitors believe strongly in visualisation and the benefits it can offer. When Chuck Norris was still competing, he used it before he fought and said that many times he scored victories on his opponents with the exact moves he had used to beat them in his mind's eye only minutes before.

SIMPLE VISUALISATION

Visualise yourself standing at the top of a large flight of stairs or entering a lift on the top floor of a building that you have been in before. Then visualise walking down the stairs or, in the case of the lift, watching the buttons light up as you descend past each floor. As you go down, your body relaxes more and more.

When you reach the bottom of the stairs or the ground floor in the lift, imagine yourself standing in your favourite place: a real place that relaxes you in real life, such as a favourite lake or park. Visualise the place in as much detail as possible, seeing all the sights, hearing all the sounds, feeling a light breeze on your face, smelling all the smells.

After a few minutes, visualise yourself standing at the bottom of the stairs or climbing back into the elevator

CUS D'AMATO

The late Cus D'Amato moulded the juvenile Mike Tyson into the phenomenon he became. The venerable D'Amato, who died in 1985, aged 77, was brought up in the tough New York district of the Bronx and was involved in boxing as a fighter, trainer and manager all his life. He guided Floyd Patterson to the world heavyweight title in 1960 – the youngest champion in history at the age of 22.

When D'Amato first set eyes on Tyson as a 13-year-old delinquent sparring with a fully grown man and hurting him, he knew he had found another special talent. Tyson went on to beat Patterson's record to win the world heavyweight champion aged 20. He credits this achievement to D'Amato who died a year before Iron Mike won the title. D'Amato gave Tyson the grounding he needed.

D'Amato's tough upbringing nurtured a unique philosophy of life and boxing which he imparted to his fighters. One lesson that became familiar to his disciples was that the fear of something is usually worse than the reality. He often told the story of the time when a well-known knife fighter challenged him to a fight to the death. They would have the fight at 7.00 the next morning in a derelict building without any witnesses so that the winner could not be charged with murder.

D'Amato could box but had no idea how to use a knife against an expert. He still accepted the challenge. He arrived an hour early at the appointed battleground the next morning to practise with an ice pick in his fist. His nerves were jangling with fear but he tried to harness it to positive effect. He knew he did not stand a chance.

Thankfully, the bully never showed. A relieved D'Amato learned from that experience that he had won a victory, not only over his adversary, but over himself. He never forgot those lessons about fear and imagination, courage and reality, and he taught them over and over to the fighters he trained.

The same philosophy applies in unarmed combat. Soldiers can turn fear around and use the adrenaline surge that comes with it to heighten their awareness in the heat of battle and maximise all their physical assets. D'Amato would have been a great general.

and beginning your ascent. As you go up, you feel more and more relaxed and energised, as though you've finished a nice, refreshing nap. When you reach the top, open your eyes. You should feel completely relaxed and totally energised.

CONCRETE VISUALISATION

This exercise is designed to accomplish two things. The first is to allow a soldier mentally to practise martial arts techniques that he may have to use some day, especially if he's trying to escape and evade. The second is to bolster self-confidence and the soldier's sense of mental resistance against the enemy, specifically by practising the martial arts techniques on imaginary captors in his mind.

Visualise yourself performing the personal combative techniques you have learned using an imaginary captor or one of your training instructors as your opponent. Visualise defeating your opponent in detail.

Each time you practise, try to add more creative elements. For example, visualise yourself making use of field-expedient weapons like rocks and sticks. Try to watch (or imagine watching) your opponent carefully during your day-to-day encounters, looking for signs of his psychology and other elements that might give you clues about the way he would fight physically. Then incorporate this information into your mental training.

Most importantly, always see yourself defeating your opponent with more speed, more efficient techniques and less use of brute force. Out-think him and then take him out.

DON'T TRY THIS AT HOME

Several of the chapters that follow give detailed descriptions of how a special forces soldier trained in military unarmed combat will handle himself in violent situations that call on those skills. But this book is not a manual, and in particular it is not a manual for unsupervised beginners. It is a book of information about trained soldiers using skills they have learned under expert instruction. They are men who understand stances, sweeps and strikes as well as how to fall safely every time. They are also men who respect the power and potential to damage that their skill gives them, and they are trained in its responsible use.

The techniques outlined are extremely dangerous and

LEFT: Troops training with cudgel sticks; they look strange but they are the safest way of training while being protected from serious injury.

can cause serious harm or even death if performed carelessly, incorrectly or without professional supervision. Tragedies can occur even when 'safety' weapons are used – a rubber knife, say, can seriously and permanently damage an eye, even when safety goggles are supposedly in use.

Yet alongside a strong respect for pain, every soldier must also foster the power to summon a ferocious aggression and direct it fully against his opponent. Aggression is a two-edged sword in unarmed combat. Too little, and the soldier is unlikely to sustain his courage and strength if the fight looks like turning against him (adrenaline levels are high during aggressive mind states and enhance physical strength). Too much, and the clarity of action that is essential in hand-to-hand fighting is lost and the soldier can start to make potentially lethal mistakes. The key goal to military training is to instil controlled aggression – aggression which can be turned on and off as needed and does not cloud thought processes. A basic aggression training exercise in almost all armies is bayonet training. Every British Army recruit, for instance, has to perform an exercise in which he advances at walking pace, screaming frenziedly, towards a suspended dummy which he then violently and persistently attacks with his bayonet-fitted rifle. The exercise is useful in that the walking-pace delivery of the attack makes it more difficult to summon aggression – aggression is produced more easily when the body is in a state of hyper activity so training officers look for the recruit's ability to change his mental outlook to one of violent intent by force of will alone.

In unarmed combat training, the danger involved with realistic exercises can help foster aggressive confidence, and the availability of full body armour specially designed for unarmed combat means that more soldiers can now practice unleashing their techniques with full power at an actual human target. Other forces use more specialist techniques. Both Spetsnaz and Korean troops practice breaking techniques, smashing bricks, wood and concrete slabs with various parts of the body. Breaking requires a total belief that the target can be smashed, as a lapse in concentration or confidence easily results in a broken hand or foot. Thus the soldier must bring together aggression and sharp technique into one, the exact mind-set required for effective unarmed combat manoeuvres. Aggression training is written into many features of military training, though making violence a controllable expression is a much more difficult quality to achieve.

CHAPTER 5

Vulnerable Areas of the Body

If an unarmed special forces soldier punches an armed opponent anywhere but in a vulnerable place he is not going to last long. If he crushes his opponent's windpipe then he has a good chance of surviving.

A severe attack to any part of the anatomy can be fatal, but in reality, the human body can be very durable. It is not an easy thing to stop once it is charged with pain-killing adrenaline. Adrenaline can build a brick wall around an opponent's body, rendering it impervious to punches and kicks. A soldier may even break his opponent's ribs or cause internal damage and still not deter him at the time of attack.

A human body is made up of hard and soft parts, some parts that bend, and some do not. In some places nerves are near the surface. To give himself a fighting chance in unarmed combat, a trained soldier focuses on striking only those body targets that are the most susceptible to damage. When a soldier is defending his life, knowledge is power – knowledge of his enemy's most vulnerable body targets. Knowing what to hit is one of the great equalisers in lop-sided encounters. The capacity for human beings to resist physical punishment can seem amazingly contradictory. One the one hand, a man or a woman's body is capable of enduring tremendous levels of injury and pain. Bones and

LEFT: **Classic kick-boxing moves can be adopted and are very useful for combat training. A soldier must learn what body parts are the most vulnerable and therefore the best to attack.**

VULNERABLE AREAS OF THE BODY

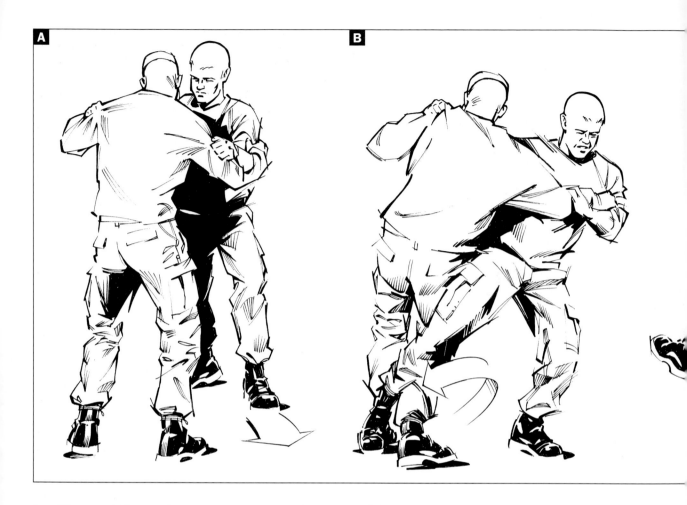

ABOVE: When a special forces soldier executes a hip throw he bends his knees as he grabs his opponent by the arms and prepares to step forwards (A). The soldier puts his leading leg behind the opponent's back leg, twists his body and raises his hip as he pulls his opponent backwards (B). The hip throw is completed as the opponent is pulled backwards and thrown to the ground (C).

muscles are durable materials and form a protective cage around the vital organs in the torso and head. Thus some boxers who have a particularly developed musculature are able to undergo 12 rounds of violent blows without succumbing to the knock-out. Soldiers often recount tales of those who sustain terrible injuries yet still continue to march or fight. Yet alongside this picture of human strength is an equal reality of human vulnerability, a reality of which the unarmed combat practitioner is acutely aware. Moveable areas such as the neck and limb joints can be

easily locked or damaged with disabling amounts of pain. The head and throat each have several points which can easily lead to unconsciousness or death if struck with appropriate force. Other areas of the body are less well covered with muscle, such as the kidneys and solar plexus, allowing an attacker to deliver blows which impact on or directly implicate vital internal organs. Lastly, the body is laced by a nerve network which if assaulted in the right place can create debilitating amounts of pain, numb and make limbs useless and even the shutdown of organs such as the heart.

When a soldier faces an opponent in a situation of hand-to-hand combat, a generalised lashing out will not be the best use of his energies. Instead he must have a clear understanding of how to use his power in the most decisive way possible by targeting the opponent's vulnerable points, which are described below.

Undoubtedly, the three most vulnerable areas to attack are the eyes, throat and jaw. A successful blow to the jaw will at the very least disorient the opponent, because of the simple fact that it shakes the brain. But the vulnerability of such areas depends largely on the situation – how easy it is for the soldier to get at them. He will, for instance, have less chance of targeting any of these three areas accurately if his opponent has grabbed him from behind. To cover every situation, the soldier makes it his business to know all the other vulnerable areas as well. There are more vulnerable spots than those listed below, but for the purposes of unarmed combat, the weak points of a man's anatomy that are most vulnerable to attack are as follows.

ATTACKING THE HEAD

Any point above his opponent's eye-line is a pretty pointless target for an unarmed soldier. To strike the skull with his fists or head is, mostly, futile. The cranium, being thick and strong to protect the brain, does just that, though it is vulnerable to kicking techniques if the assailant is horizontal.

A blow to the back of the head with a fist, however, can produce shock, concussion or even death. The temple is, of course, very vulnerable. A backhand blow, a punch or kick can lead to serious injury. But it usually takes pin-point accuracy to attack the temple effectively.

Punches or blows with the edge of the hand that affect the frontal lobe area of the brain produce shock, concussion, bleeding and unconsciousness. The classic punch to the jaw can do this, and it is hard to beat. Delivered by a skilled boxer it can put a man down for hours. The force of the blow on the point of the chin causes a 'knock-out'. This is due to the fact that the rotation of the head under the blow causes the brain to strike the inside of the skull wall, producing localised brain damage and disorientation, literally shaking the brain.

The jaw is a prime target for a good fighter. Not because it causes pain or fractures, but because if struck correctly, it causes unconsciousness, which in a life-or-death hand-to-hand fight, is the optimum goal, especially if a soldier is facing more than one opponent. The jaw line is replete with nerve clusters, particularly true of three inches either side of the jaw point. If struck hard these produce an overall numbness and shock which can easily lead to unconsciousness.

The same result can be achieved by a blow from the heel of the hand, which packs immense power. Using the heel of the hand is much easier for those inexperienced in boxing, because it has more of an element of surprise and it can be used from a shorter starting distance. Accuracy is of the essence if a knock is to result.

The face is naturally incredibly vulnerable to being struck. Punching to the temples is a particularly dangerous attack, as the limited bone covering of this point means that the brain much more directly receives the force of the blow, haemorrhaging being a likely result.

Bringing the head close to the teeth exposes the nose and the ears to being bitten, a form of attack which can bring enormous amounts of pain and very heavy blood loss if doggedly pursued. Yet human teeth are also the locus for a massive range of bacteria. If a head butt (or a fist for that matter) shatters the opponent's teeth, lacerations to the attacker can occur from the broken enamel edges and infection and blood poisoning can be the result, with the

BELOW: A simple throwing technique from behind involves the soldier stealthily getting behind his opponent and using the right hand to grab the crotch and the left to grab the shoulder or collar.

BELOW: The opponent is caught unawares and is pulled backwards with the right hand whilst being pushed forwards with the left. The opponent will fall to the ground face first.

potential to also contract saliva-borne diseases (a serious consideration in tropical parts of the world or regions which suffer from low standards of sanitation and hygiene).

The eyes are one of the most vulnerable, accessible and sensitive parts of the human anatomy. They can be scraped, poked or gouged using the fingers. Any connection between finger and eye will cause extreme pain and, more often than not, stop an opponent completely. The attack can collapse an eye-ball, lacerate an eye-lid or in some cases knock an eye-ball completely out of its socket.

An alert soldier is always aware of anything unusual or unexpected that can be done to confuse an opponent. If the soldier can throw dirt in his eyes, or hit him with any object that readily comes to hand or create any other diversion, he has won an advantage.

Because the nose protrudes from the face, it is an obvious target. Grappling at close quarters, a soldier may find it the easiest part of the enemy's facial anatomy to sink his teeth into. When an enemy has the soldier in a rear bear hug the enemy's nose is a very vulnerable target for a rear head butt.

A strong opponent can often shake off such an attack and carry on. Pain and watery eyes are commonly the only outcome, but a severe attack to the nose can sometimes be fatal. An edge of the hand blow or kick delivered at the point where the nose joins the bony structure of the brow can crush the most fragile part of the bony structure. It can lead to unconsciousness and even death from brain haemorrhage. A blow with the edge of the hand directed underneath the nose in an upward direction toward the forehead can be lethal, causing crushing of the frontal bones, unconsciousness and brain haemorrhage.

Attacks to the ears, especially when both ears are attacked together, can be potentially fatal if unconsciousness and concussion follow. In the ear concussion blow, the soldier approaches his opponent from the rear. Concussion and a rupture of the eardrums can be caused by cupping both hands and simultaneously striking them against his ears. The ear drums may rupture, because large amounts of air are forced into the internal canal of the ear. In reality, this seldom happens, though the pain inflicted by such an attack often leaves the victim disoriented and this makes

LEFT: A soldier's leg is caught as he executes a high front kick at an opponent during training. This illustrates that only the fastest and most flexible soldiers should attempt kicking anywhere above the waist.

him an easier subject to overpower. This attack can sometimes stop an assailant long enough to allow the soldier to take control of him.

The ear can also be ripped by gripping and pulling, though this can be difficult if it is sweaty. A more effective attack against the ear is to bite it, causing panic and extreme pain. This can disrupt even the most vicious attack by an opponent at close quarters. Located just behind the ears is the bony promontory called the mastoid process. If hit hard, the mastoid process will affect the opponent's sense of balance by disrupting the inner ear and can even result in unconsciousness.

ATTACKS TO THE THROAT AND THE NECK

In unarmed combat a soldier will almost always try to manoeuvre himself into a position where he can go for the throat – 'vulnerable' is not a descriptive enough word for this accessible and susceptible area. It is only partially protected by the jaw and neck muscles, and accuracy alone is enough to strike a telling blow. Soldiers trained in unarmed combat use chopping and straight finger strikes most effective against this target. A strong, accurate attack may cause any one of a myriad of injuries.

For close-in fighting, grabbing the windpipe around the Adam's apple and squeezing the larynx tightly may cause choking and, in the extreme, unconsciousness. A blow with the edge of the hand across the windpipe causes temporary and sometimes permanent blackout. The blow has a similar effect to crushing a strip of copper tubing with a sharp-edged instrument. The effect can be gauged by placing your thumb in the small hollow at the base of your throat and pressing gently.

Blows on the sides of the throat and on the large cords at the back of the neck can cause dislocation, concussion and even a break. Running down both sides of the neck about one inch either side of the trachea are the vagus nerves, vital cranial nerves which supply the pharynx, larynx, oesophagus, stomach, intestines, heart, lungs and abdominal organs. Special forces soldiers are often taught to strike the vagus nerves with a double blow as a potentially lethal attack. If the vagus nerves are struck in this way, heartbeat and breathing are severely interrupted by the altered nervous signals and death can result. Inadvertent vagus nerve strikes are one of the predominant causes of accidental death during martial arts competitions, and these points are so vulnerable that there have even been recorded cases of individuals dying

ATTACKS TO THE ARMS AND LEGS

Although they are protected by surrounding muscle, all limb joints – finger, elbow, shoulder and knee – are vulnerable to attack. On the shoulder joint, a punch or an elbow produces extreme pain. A punch or kick to the elbow joint can be very painful too. Knees can be easily attacked with kicking techniques, if a soldier is proficient enough with his feet to find the necessary accuracy. However, it takes no skill at all to bend back an assailant's fingers. Nature made these joints bend one way only; so if they are forced in the opposite direction, they will either break or cause an opponent to go down. The fore-arms in particular are host to some major nerve pathways, and blows with the fist anywhere on the inside of the arm can produce tingling numbness which deadens the effectiveness of the opponent's punching and striking capability.

The elbows have a short and fast swing radius and terminate in a solid bone point. This point is incredibly strong, much more so than the many small and fragile bones contained in the hand. Furthermore, a strike with the hand has to cope with shock being transmitted through the wrist, elbow and shoulder joints, whereas an elbow strike keeps all its shock unproblematically to the single bone of the upper arm and the large shoulder and back muscles. Elbows are consequently one of the most potent tools in the soldier's store.

The knees, because of their hinge structure – as any footballer will testify – are particularly susceptible to hard blows, especially those struck by the feet. If you are kicked from behind on the back of your knees in a fight, you will fold up off balance and may be finished off that much faster. Blows or kicks delivered directly at the knee cap from the front or directly from the right or left side of the knee when the leg is straight can easily break or dislodge the patella (the knee-cap) or dislocate the connection between the femur and the tibia bones. The subsequent loss of mobility gives the soldier an ideal opening to conclude his attacks. Even light blows delivered in this manner cause dislocations of tendons and nerves. They are common amongst footballers, known as 'football knee'.

through receiving over-energetic kissing of the neck area from their lover! Running alongside the vagus nerves, the neck also contains major blood vessels which supply the brain. If these are forcibly constricted unconsciousness will result in a few seconds, unlike a stranglehold to the throat which only cuts off breathing and can take up to a minute to produce compliance. Very few men can withstand edge of the hand blows on these spots. A blow to the collarbone with the side of the fist or edge of the hand brings about fracturing and sharp pain.

The knees are a particularly effective area to attack on larger men, as the extra weight that they carry tends to make for weaker knee joints than in smaller people. Kicking the shins with the toe or scraping with the arch of the foot or a heel kick produces crippling pain, fracturing, and sometimes shock. A stomp on the instep and arch is also very painful and can fracture bones. If accurate kicking is not possible, then generalised blows to the thigh muscles using the shin bone can be an invaluable way of gaining a fighting advantage. Most people are familiar with the dead-leg sensation, and if inflicted repeatedly then the opponent soon becomes less nimble in his movements and actions.

ATTACKING THE TRUNK OF THE BODY

An experienced soldier never expends energy on non-vulnerable areas like the back, chest and shoulders. While some of these areas do conceal major organs that may be susceptible to attack, they are too well protected by major muscle groups to penetrate. He is much more likely to go for the testicles, the most vulnerable and sensitive part of a man's body.

Grabbing the crotch from behind, for example, is extremely simple and reliable. This technique can be used under any conditions against an armed and dangerous opponent regardless of his strength, size or weapon. The soldier gets right up behind him stealthily and uses the right hand to grab the crotch and the left to grab the shoulder or collar. The opponent is pulled backwards with the right hand while being pulled forwards with the left. If he tears loose, he is tripped or knocked down.

In the less likely case of the soldier standing beside his opponent, the soldier clenches his fist and strikes the opponent in the testicles with the hand nearest his body. This will make him bend forward for the follow-up, which can be an edge of the hand blow at the back of his neck or base of the skull, or a kick in the face.

Any foot or hand blow delivered to the crotch will enable the weakest man to knock the strongest senseless or to disable him to a point where he is easily finished off by some other means. The strongest holds can be broken at any time by grasping an opponent's testicles and pulling, crushing and twisting them. A strong kick to this area may rupture the urinary bladder, causing shock, internal bleeding or thrombosis, or even a clot in a main vein which could ultimately lodge in the lungs causing death. If no other target is available a trained soldier will always

NINJITSU

The acute understanding of the human body's vulnerable points was developed perhaps better than any other martial arts group by the legendary Ninja, one of the first militaristic groupings to be defined by their exceptional unarmed combat skills. Meaning 'the art of espionage', Ninjitsu originated over 800 years ago in the mountainous Iga and Koga regions of Japan. During this period of Japan's history, Japan's peasant population was subservient to the Samurai class of warrior, who were in turn loyal to their lord, the Shogun. The Ninja came together as those who either refused to serve the Samurai, or were themselves former Samurai whose lord had been killed in battle. In their isolated and illegal community, the Ninja's training in deadly martial arts was exceptional and comprehensive and would serve them well in what became their primary role: elite mercenaries for hire by whoever had money and cause. Ninja specialities were primarily espionage, sabotage and assassination, with lethal skills in unarmed combat, weaponry and explosives. Training also involved a broad education in the arts and sciences to help them mix with any society they encountered in their covert missions.

The Ninja separated into various clans and from the thirteenth century each clan tended to demonstrate a specialism in one field of combat or espionage. However, all Ninja had a mastery of unarmed combat techniques, especially in relation to the silent disposal of sentries and significant human targets. Consequently, Ninjitsu contained a prodigious knowledge of strangulation holds, neck breaks, nerve strikes and lethal punches which, combined with their fully justified reputation for stealth and ruthlessness, made them much feared.

Though the Ninja name continues today in the many martial arts clubs around the world dedicated to the practice of Ninjitsu, especially in the United States, the authentic Ninja no longer exist. Various military forces, however, have taken interest in Ninjitsu unarmed techniques, especially those involving ambush, silent killing and escape. Again, interest is strongest in the US, and the total practicality of purpose behind Ninjitsu means that its fighting skills (as much as we genuinely know about them) have been studied by many elite units.

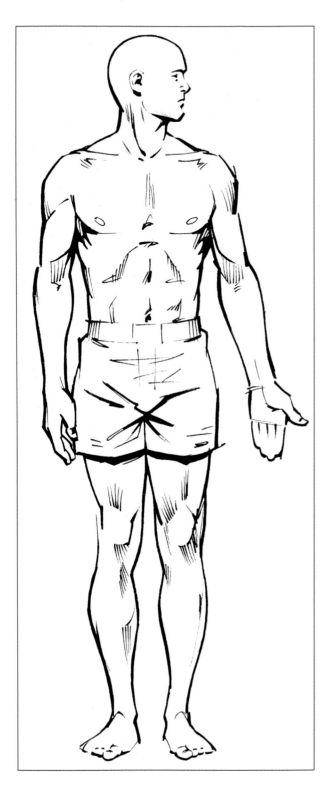

consider this worth a try. Yet despite the evident effectiveness of a blow to the crotch it should be attempted with some care. The shock reaction of a blow in this area often causes a massive adrenaline rush in the recipient which can give him an enormous burst of violent energy for three or four seconds until the pain becomes overwhelming. This is naturally a particularly dangerous time for the attacker and thus an attack to the groin must be part to the systematic series of attacks to disallow the opponent any real room for response.

The main muscle cords and nerves of the body branch out from the base of the spine at a point very near the surface. In this area, a sharp sudden blow has a great stunning effect which is why it is ruled a foul shot in boxing. The entire section across the back just above the base of the spine, including the right and left kidney, is sensitive to this form of attack. Both the lower spine and kidneys have little muscle protection in this area and consequently experience much greater pain if struck.

Slightly below the navel is another vulnerable spot, which, if hit effectively enough, will cause unconsciousness. However, it is not always easy to find this spot. It is not the same as a blow to the solar plexus, which is delivered above the navel, just under the rib cage. A severe attack to the solar plexus can cause anything from critical liver damage to a torn gall bladder or even a complete rupture of the stomach, which may culminate in massive internal bleeding. Due to severe shock or blood loss this can end in death. The solar plexus, situated directly in the

LEFT: Major target areas are the head, groin, torso and neck. These areas are attacked violently and swiftly as there are no second chances.

TARGET AREAS

The aim of a soldier engaged in unarmed combat is to use the fighting techniques at his disposal to cause as much damage to the opponent's body as he can, as quickly possible. To make it possible for him to do this, his training gives him a thorough knowledge of the body's major target areas. They include points on the head, groin, torso, neck and extremities. Whichever of these areas the soldier can get at are areas that he will attack instantly and with violence, without any expectation of having second chances.

centre of the chest at the fork of the rib cage, is especially vulnerable to a heavy punch owing to it being the only place on the human chest that is not covered by either muscle or bone. More realistically, the soldier is likely to knock the wind out of his opponent with a blow to the solar plexis, and this will give him the opportunity to carry on undeterred to the next move in his attack. If attacking the ribs, it is often best to punch at the base of the rib cage targeting what are known as the floating ribs. These are the two lowest ribs and have no direct or indirect attachment to the sternum. Thus they are easily bent inwards by a punch, either breaking or forcing the diaphragm inwards and causing the loss of respiratory control in the opponent.

VITAL PRESSURE POINTS

There are numerous pressure points on the body where

ABOVE: The soldier on the left is demonstrating a classic X-block against a front kick. Crossing his arms at the wrist, he traps the attacker's kick in the fork made by his arms and stops it from fully extending and gathering power.

severe pain is felt when certain nerve centres are pressed. Such attacks do not have any permanent damaging effects, though, and can only be used to break holds. Other targets mentioned above are better for this purpose.

However, one nerve centre is worth mentioning above others. If a man is lying on the ground, feigning death or unconsciousness and a soldier wants to stir him, the soldier should lean over him and using the middle fingers press on each side of the head into the points of his skull where the jaw bone is hinged. Pressing in and up towards the top of the head will cause such pain that no man can stand it. He will give up his pretense instantly.

CHAPTER 6

Punching and Kicking

The body has many natural weapons, and it is imperative for a soldier to learn to use them all to maximum potential. Ground fighting, defending against a knife attack and general unarmed combat are all the same for a soldier: he is attacked and he must survive.

A soldier must learn to beat his opponent in an unarmed combat situation in any manner. Within instants he may move from fighting with his fists to head-butting at close quarters or clawing with his fingers and jabbing with his knees on the ground at an opponent who is attempting to apply a stranglehold.

From the ideal hand-to-hand combat fighting range, however, the intermediate range just outside grappling distance, he will generally be able to strike only with his hands and feet. This is the distance from which he can easily see what he is doing and see what his opponent is trying to do. From here he can punch or kick his opponent's body, and punch, possibly even kick, his head, where accurate blows to the jaw will cause disorientation or unconsciousness.

Punching the opponent may continue to be a priority, even after the opponent is subdued. If the soldier is taking the man captive, a come-along method may be necessary

LEFT: Spetsnaz soldiers take training to the extreme. Kicking an opponent is preferable to close-quarters combat fighting: the soldier can see what he is doing more clearly and a kick to the head or the groin area can disable an opponent for long enough to take action.

85

LEFT: As a punch, the finger jab is generally used as an 'opener', a lead punch that lacks real power, but is very good for causing irritation and disorientation in an opponent through the stinging pain inflicted.

ABOVE: A jab helps make openings for the bigger punches that might follow and can be delivered with finger strike or clawhand. This move needs to be effected with great speed.

to take him to the destination point. There are no completely effective bare-handed come-alongs. The victim may well be prepared to hurt himself to break free, because he is so desperate to escape. Often, the only way to prevent a prisoner causing trouble when he is being taken in over any distance is to keep him in a perpetual state of semi-consciousness by edge of the hand blows to the neck, short jabs on the chin, or by any means that will keep his mental processes foggy.

BLOWS USING THE HEEL OF THE HAND

A soldier's best blows using the hands are often delivered with the flat or heel of the hand or the edge of the hand. Blows struck with the fist, such as uppercuts, hooks and jabs, are most effective when the user is experienced in boxing and its allied sports. It can take months to learn how to deliver a clinical knockout blow with either fist, but the basic boxing techniques can be mastered in the first few sessions. What really matters is how long a special forces soldier spends developing the speed and power of each skill.

The heel-of-the-hand blow to the jaw is the simplest and most effective of all blows of this type, and when it is used in conjunction with a kick in the groin, which causes an opponent to bend forwards, it will often result in a severe neck injury, possibly a fracture. The beauty of using this blow is its simplicity. In using the closed-fist boxing technique, a man not used to using his fists may easily break a finger or bone in his hand or cut himself on his opponent's face.

THE CHIN JAB

This is an extremely effective blow, delivered up and under the chin with the heel of the palm. The fingers are extended, to give the palm rigidity. The more directly underneath the chin the blow falls, the more power it packs. It is executed with a bent elbow and a great deal of body weight to maximise impact.

The further forward the enemy soldier's chin is extended at the time of the blow, the more devastating the result. If a knee is thrust into his groin to start with, his body will automatically bend forwards, creating a perfect opportunity for this particular blow. The jab results in unconsciousness and possible neck fracture or spinal injury if delivered with sufficient force.

This blow can be a real surprise to the recipient, because the striker's arm or hand does not have to draw back before execution. The arm can be hanging at the side, fingers hooked in a belt, hand resting on lapel, or in any other nonchalant position. An average man is capable of a knock-out with only six inches (150 mm) of travelling distance from the start of the blow to the point of impact. This is most useful in close quarters where time, space or circumstances do not allow the hand and arm to be withdrawn for a long shot.

A neck fracture can be achieved by gripping the opponent's belt with one hand and using it to jerk him forwards at the moment of the other hand strikes. A soldier will often use the fingers of the striking hand on the opponent's eyes following the blow.

A chin jab followed by a trip can be used to down an enemy while passing him by, taking advantage of the element of surprise. This is a very simple and effective move which can be executed without any suspicious warning movements. As the soldier passes his opponent on the left side, when he is directly opposite to him, he places his right leg in the rear of his opponent's right and executes a chin jab from a position of hands at side. He will be down and out. The leg in the rear has the effect of making the body come down with more force.

PUNCHING

Hands can be used to punch in any direction with power. The knuckles are, when the fist is clenched, an extremely solid and durable element. When engaged by the transferred body weight, they become devastatingly destructive as an attacking tool. The fact that hands have an acute sense of touch also helps. The boxing punch of a left or right hook is the most effective way of using human hands.

Soldiers who rely on hand speed and power practise extensively and probably have strong boxing backgrounds in the army. They concentrate on accuracy and speed over power. Speed and power are not usually enough to knock out an adversary without accuracy. (Mike Tyson does not attribute his phenomenal first round knockout ratio just to power but also to his speed, and mainly to his accuracy.)

As a punch, the jab is generally used as an 'opener', a lead punch that lacks real power, but is very good for causing irritation and disorientation in an opponent through the stinging pain inflicted. A jab helps make openings for the bigger punches that might follow and can be delivered with a finger strike or clawhand. The same attack used with

RIGHT: Thrown from the leading leg and aimed, ultimately, at the jaw, the uppercut can be a damaging shot. For maximum power, the soldier places his right hip forward and to the opponent's left before he strikes, slightly bending at the knees so that he is just below the target.

an open hand transforms an irritating technique into a stopping one. This is attained by either clawing the hand or by coupling the fingers together to poke the eyes.

THE LEFT HOOK

Thrown with a clenched fist by a right-handed person off the leading left leg and aimed at the opponent's jaw, and delivered with a sufficient transfer of body weight, this is a very powerful punch. A very similar blow can be delivered using the same technique, but with the heel of the palm.

As any boxer will testify, the best punches start at the tip of the toes and are delivered by transferring body weight through legs, torso, shoulder, arm and finally fist. Footwork is as important as the arm movement. The best punches come when the feet are planted and knees bent slightly. Throwing a hook on the move rarely has the desired effect, because the soldier's balance is likely to be all wrong and getting the full body weight behind it is very difficult.

All hooking punches are thrown in the same style as a slap, attacking with knuckles as opposed to the flat of the hand. Perfect execution is vital because, when connecting with anything other than the knuckles of a clenched fist, it is easy to damage your hand. Even seasoned boxers hurt their gloved hands; so it can easily happen to a less experienced fighter with bare knuckles.

For maximum power, expert punchers push their right hip forward and slightly to the left before the strike. As they throw the left fist towards the target, they twist their left hip sharply across and to the right, following the path of their punch. This hip movement ensures maximum weight transference into the punch.

THE LEFT UPPERCUT

Thrown from the leading left leg and aimed ultimately at the jaw, the left uppercut is a damaging shot when correctly employed. For maximum power, the soldier places his right hip forward and to the left before he strikes, slightly bending at the knees so that he is just below the target. He throws his left fist upwards, twisting the fist on impact with the jaw so that the palm is facing inward to his own body. Simultaneously, he pushes upwards from a crouched position, thrusting the left hip forward and upwards,

following the path of the punch. On connection with the jaw, he follows through with the punch and hip for maximum effect. He uses the same technique for the palm heel.

THE RIGHT CROSS

The right cross is a very powerful punch using all of the striker's weight when correctly executed. It is thrown from the back with the right hand from a left-leg leading stance.

The striker throws the right fist towards the jaw, simultaneously thrusting his right hip forward and in the direction of the punch. With a finger strike, claw or palm heel, the target area is more likely to be the eyes than the jaw.

BLOWS USING THE EDGE OF THE HAND

Highly effective blows are delivered with the edge of the hand, because it can be used on vulnerable spots of the

LEFT: The flying kick straight ahead. Kicks delivered from a leap are extremely effective if executed accurately and with sufficient determination to succeed.

body which are not as susceptible to blows from the fist or heel of the hand.

The edge-of-the-hand blow is delivered with the fingers extended, close together, thumb upright and wrist locked. The striking surface is the cushioned part of the hand between the base of the little finger and the edge of the palm where it joins the wrist, as in a 'karate chop'. The thumb is raised to an upright position because this automatically extends the fingers and prevents the hand from clenching.

The striking surface is well padded and its length, varying with the size of different hands, is roughly 3 inches (75mm). The thickness of the palm in most cases is about one inch (25mm). That small area of the hand can be

highly effective when used correctly.

Unlike a clenched fist which covers a bigger area, the edge-of-the-hand blow gives a sharp-edged effect, more likely to cause a break, fracture or concussion because of the force delivered on a relatively small area.

The blow is made with the elbow bent, thus utilising body weight behind it, and delivered with a sharp chopping motion. This localises the force of the blow in a small area. If the hand is not quickly drawn back, a great deal of the striking power is expended over a larger area, so becoming less effective.

This blow can be delivered with either hand in a downward direction or horizontally with the palm down as in a backhand tennis or sabre stroke. The best position in

BELOW: The flying kick from the side. There is little margin for error with this technique and even a slight mistake can result in a soldier hurting himself far more than his opponent.

which to use the horizontal edge-of-the-hand blow is with the foot forward, so that the body weight can fully get behind the blow. The reverse foot position has a lessened effect.

KICKING

Effective kicking is a difficult talent to learn, requiring balance, a certain degree of flexibility and good technique to avoid whiplash injuries to knee joints or a broken foot. Most military forces around the world recognise this and few teach advanced kicking techniques apart from the more easily trained blows using short kicks to the shins, knees or groin. There are exceptions to this of course. Soldiers of North and South Korea receive instruction in the very kick-based martial art of taekwondo, and often become extremely capable (and flexible) combat kickers who are capable of smashing bricks with head-high round-house or spinning kicks. Likewise, Russian Spetsnaz special forces soldiers trained in Combat Sambo can also wreak formidable damage to the head and chest with a boot-clad foot. However, the spectacular demonstration kicks these units present at military shows and exercises are often thoroughly inadvisable in actual combat situations, primarily because they leave the kicker in a physically vulnerable posture if he doesnt put his opponent down with the technique.

Feet may be used to attack from front, side, back or round ways to any part of the opponent's anatomy. They are especially effective for attacking the opponent's lower regions. The best targets are the lower abdominal regions, – including the pubic bone and the groin – the knees and the shins.

The best tactic when helping a comrade caught in a chokehold is often to kick the assailant. Kicks to the head are the best, because the opponent may be wearing a flak jacket, which gives protection to the body. If the opponent is choking your comrade it is best not to shove or grapple.

Kicks delivered from a leap are extremely effective if executed with great accuracy and commitment for success. However, even a slight mistake can result in the attacking soldier hurting himself far more than his opponent.

RIGHT: **The roundhouse kick. Lift the attacking knee high and to the side (A), and by pivoting on the supporting leg quickly kick the opponent (B). Striking with the ball of the foot is the best way of maximising impact – any target below the chest can hurt.**

A

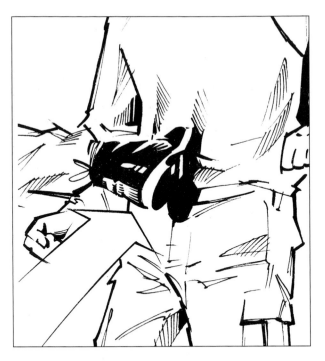

ABOVE: Feet may be used to attack from the front, side or back to any part of the opponent's anatomy. They are especially useful for attacking the opponent's lower regions. The best targets are the lower abdominal region.

Kicking is absolutely the hardest unarmed combat skill to develop. People are comfortable walking on two feet, but when they leave the ground for something like kicking, alarms go off in the head and the body becomes unbalanced. But there are some almost natural exceptions.

Both children and adults learn certain kinds of kicks by playing with balls – footballs, tennis balls, beach balls – and with such a wide exposure to martial arts today, children can also be seen throwing their version of martial arts kicks when they're playing with their friends. The enduring popularity of Bruce Lee, Chuck Norris and Jackie Chan films along with the mainstream 'action men' like Sly Stallone and Bruce Willis keeps interest high. These undisciplined and untrained kicks seem natural to the boys who throw them and it is this same spirit that is often used by the training soldier.

Many instructors will introduce a soldier to kicking by allowing him to block a punch and then kick the opponent in the knee or groin. The general train of thought is that they should not be shown a specific way of doing it, but force them to find the technique themselves. This method trains the leg as a much more natural reflexive weapon.

The rationale behind this training is to prevent the soldier from becoming too preoccupied with the one-two-three-four mentality of doing a proper front, side or roundhouse kick. Most soldiers have tremendously strong legs from regular rucksack marching and swimming, so the natural kicks tend to have adequate power for stopping an attacker.

A kick delivered toe foremost and aimed at a narrow target is very risky. The slightest move on the opponent's part may cause the soldier to miss, and leave him off-balance and wide open to retaliation. Only a soldier with exceptionally good footwork and balance, or one very experienced in a martial art, will try to kick a standing opponent at any point above knee height unless the opponent's hands are otherwise engaged.

The most effective technique is to kick with either the inside or the outside of the foot. This blow, delivered with the aid of heavy footwear, gives a striking surface of the length of the foot from heel to toe. When properly delivered it allows the kicker to keep his balance in case of a miss or a merely glancing blow.

FRONT AND SIDE KICKS

The kick is most effective when delivered from the front directly to or a few inches below the knee cap. For best results, a soldier will allow the foot to scrape down, putting the weight at the finish across the ankle joint. The effect is that it bruises the tender shin bones and crushes the small bones of the foot, which are very tender and unprotected.

When this blow is delivered properly, the opponent's knee may pop out of its socket or, if the knee is in a slightly flexed position – not getting the full weight of the blow against its hinge – the foot will bear the brunt of the kick by way of the follow-up down the shin. It will be crushed and made completely useless. The opponent will topple to the ground, leaving him open for an easy kick to any exposed vulnerable part of the body.

The same kicking blow against the knee from the side will have equal effect as the one from the front. A vicious kick on the shins will cause the strongest man to lurch forward and stick out his chin, leaving him open for a chin jab or uppercut.

The coup de grace is applied once your opponent is downed with a forceful kick. The best areas to aim for with the toe, heel or foot are the mid-section, throat area or

temples. When using the heel to finish off an opponent, exponents find it is best to use one foot only, driving it into the rib section or other vulnerable area. This allows them to maintain better balance than they could if they jumped on their opponent with both heels. Using both legs is particularly dangerous if the ground is uneven or the fallen man rolls. The danger is that you will lose your balance and go to ground with him.

THE ROUNDHOUSE KICK

The roundhouse kick is very powerful and effective, but requires much more skill than the front kick. Any target below the chest is a good bet, particularly the ribs, kidneys, lower abdomen, groin, testicles, thighs and shins. Technique is important here – the higher the target area aimed for with this kick the more danger there is of impaired balance and a slow recovery.

The attacking part of the foot can be the instep or the

ABOVE: US Marines boxing during free time on the flight deck of the USS *Trenton*. This was part of Field Training Exercise Solid Shield in 1987; this was a large scale joint exercise of over 22,000 US military members of the US Army, Navy, Air Force and Marine Corps. It took place along the Atlantic coast and Central America.

ball of the foot. If it is the ball of the foot, then the toes and foot are pulled back so that on impact with the target the heel is higher than the toes. If it is the instep, the toes and ankle are pushed forward and the strike is made with the bone at the front of the foot.

To get maximum impact, the knee of the attacking leg is lifted high and to the side and the attacking leg is thrown around and into the target by pivoting on the supporting leg and thrusting the hips behind the technique on impact. After contact with the target the leg is quickly retracted by pivoting back on the supporting leg and pulling the hips back to their original position.

CHAPTER 7

Blocks Against Punches and Kicks

Defensive blocking using the arm with the forearm up, employed against hand blows and kicks, is a vital part of unarmed combat. The soldier's goal is not just to defend against an attack, but to put himself in a position to counter-attack.

D efensive blocking is a vital part of unarmed combat. The soldier's basic stance for this is with the knees slightly bent, spread to about the shoulders' width; arms bent at the elbows, with the hands made into fists. As with all defensive skills, the soldier's goal is not just to defend against an attack, but to put himself in a position to counter-attack. Thus a counter-attack is often an integral part of the sequence he will have drilled as his choice of response to a given attack.

Defensive movements should not break the balance of the basic warrior stance. While defending against an attack, the defending arm – the lead arm – moves out of position only enough to engage the attack. The non-defending arm maintains its position. Because the lead hand is closest to

LEFT: This staged shot demonstrates the level of skill required when employing defensive blocks. One of the key features of a defensive movement is balance: the soldier should not overbalance while defending against an attack.

the opponent, it assumes most of the defensive duties. The rear hand backs up the lead hand and blocks incoming attacks to the right side of the head and torso.

It is best to block or parry on an angle so that the full force of an attack is not directly opposed. Blocking or parrying lessens the force of impact, allows better opportunity for a counter-attack and protects the defensive zone. (The 'defensive zone' is the area an attack must enter to cause damage.) To ensure success, blocking moves are executed with as much speed and force as possible.

A soldier would have to break the basic warrior stance in order to react to an attack delivered from outside the defensive zone. If he lived to regret such a move, he would be lucky, for in making it he would leave himself less able to engage the opponent and would expose himself to a secondary attack. A well-trained soldier does not defend against attacks that are delivered outside the defensive zone.

Of course, the best form of block in any unarmed combat action is simply not to be where the punch or kick is thrown. Conventional blocking is not without cost. Repeated clashing of arms is a tiring activity, and can lead to numbed or even damaged limbs which impair the successful resolution of the fight. Ducking or side-stepping can be much more viable options as long as the soldier still manages to retain his position for attack. However, sometimes rough terrain or constricted environments (such as inside buildings) do not permit such evasions, and thus blocking becomes an important and necessary skill.

DEFENCE FOR A LEAD-HAND PUNCH

If the opponent attacks with a lead-hand punch, the soldier parries with his rear hand to repel the attack. The key to this defence lies in his rapid response. To defend against a lead-hand punch he:

- executes a rear-hand parry while sliding forwards with the lead foot,
- hooks his left arm over the opponent's right shoulder while moving his right hand to the back of the opponent's neck to lock and control the opponent's right arm,
- uses both his arms to apply pressure and force the opponent's head down,
- executes a knee strike to the face,
- grabs the opponent behind the neck, rotates his hips and

executes a leg sweep taking the opponent to the ground,
- executes a heel stomp to the opponent's head as a finishing technique.

DEFENCE FOR A REAR-HAND PUNCH

If the opponent attacks with a rear-hand punch, the soldier:

- executes an outside block with his lead hand,
- steps in with his rear foot and executes a forearm strike to the opponent's elbow with the inside of his rear forearm (this will damage the elbow),
- executes an elbow strike to the opponent's ribs,
- wrap his forearm and bicep around the opponent's upper arm,
- rotates his hips and upper body and drives the opponent to the ground (to provide leverage for this movement, the soldier grips the opponent's injured upper arm, pulls on it and turns the opponent over his hips and upper thigh),
- executes a heel stomp to the opponent's head as a finishing technique.

DEFENCE FOR AN UPPERCUT PUNCH

If the opponent attacks with an uppercut punch, the soldier then:

- executes a low block with his lead hand,
- strikes the inside of his opponent's elbow with the palm of his rear hand (not to cause damage but to create an opening between his arm and torso),
- moves his lead hand through the opening while his rear hand moves to the back of the opponent's neck to control the upper torso,
- uses both his arms to apply pressure and force the opponent's head down,
- executes a knee strike to the opponent's face,
- grabs the opponent behind the neck, rotates his hips and executes a leg sweep taking the opponent to the ground,
- uses a heel stomp as a finishing technique.

RIGHT: The forearm can be used to cover the head and torso from a wide range of attacks. From a guard position, the forearm can be rapidly snatched across the body to provide either an outer block (A) useful for countering swinging punches to the head and an inner block (B) good for countering jabs to face and body.

DEFENCE FOR A FRONT KICK

If the opponent attacks with a front kick, the most effective counter is to parry with the lead hand to repel the attack, then:

- grab the back of the opponent's collar with the rear hand,
- execute a rear-leg side kick to the opponent's knee, taking him to his knees,
- execute an eye gouge with lead hand,
- force the opponent's head back, exposing the throat,
- execute a knifehand (edge-of-the-hand) strike to the opponent's throat as a finishing technique.

OTHER BLOCKS FOR INTERMEDIATE-RANGE FIGHTING

The high block defends against overhead attacks. To execute the high block a soldier:

- closes his hand to prevent finger injuries,
- snaps his forearm up,
- bends his elbow,
- applies tension to both his elbow and shoulder.

The low block defends against attacks to the soldier's mid-section and groin. To execute the low block, he:

- closes his hand to protect his fingers,

LEFT: The double block is one of the strongest blocks in unarmed combat. Both forearms are driven into the attacker's arms as it swings towards the head, and from this position it is easy to follow up with chops to the throat and wristlocks.

- snaps his forearm down the front of his body to engage the attack,
- applies tension to his elbow and shoulder.

Again, the opponent strikes the outside of the soldier's forearm.

The outside block defends against attacks directed at the soldier's upper body from the outside and straight-in attacks directed at his upper body. To execute the outside block the soldier:

- closes his hand to protect his fingers,
- snaps his blocking arm to the outside of his body,
- engages the attack,
- ensures that the attack does not drive his defending arm into his opponent's body or head,
- applies tension to his elbow and shoulder.

The inside block defends against straight-in attacks directed at the soldier's upper body. To execute the inside block he:

- closes his hand to protect his fingers,
- snaps his forearm toward the inside of his body,
- applies tension to his elbow and shoulder.

THE LEG BLOCK AND DOUBLE BLOCK

The leg block defends against low-level kicks to the soldier's groin and the joints of his lead leg. By countering an opponent's low-level kick with a leg block, the soldier's defensive posture is not compromised. To execute the leg block, he raises the knee of his lead leg. The opponent should strike his lead leg.

The double block is used to stop side-slashing attacks. Against a right-handed attack, the soldier executes this block by raising his clenched fists to either side of his face and placing his elbows in front of his chest and his body perpendicular to the attacker's.

The heel-palm block is usually used as a powerful strike, but it can also be used to push an attacker to the ground by driving him backward and down to the ground before finally incapacitating him.

BODY CONDITIONING

Successful blocking and countering requires a body strong enough to absorb the hard clash of bone and muscle without the fighters ability to continue to use his limbs being impaired. Conditioning the body to handle such violent contact is a necessary, though much neglected, practice. Conditioning essentially involves using specialised equipment or drills to toughen skin and muscle and thus allow the conditioned fighter to have a greatly increased resistance to pain. Hands are an obvious area for conditioning. Punchbag training alone, first using wraps then bare fists, can go a long way to making the knuckles harden and become less susceptible to stripping when punching a target. Some martial artists and soldiers also practice exercises such as punching bowls of sand or small stones or a string-covered oak post (known as a makiwara) to increase hardening, though such exercises are little to be seen outside the East. As forearms are the major tool of blocking, their conditioning is advisable and is probably one of the most practised techniques. One of the simplest and most productive methods of achieving this is for two people to face each other and repeat a sequence of arm clashes, varying the strike surface with each blow so that the whole forearm is conditioned. The power behind the strikes is gradually increased over weeks and months as the participant's pain tolerance grows. This technique is used by boxers as a training technique. A final conditioning zone is the legs, or more particularly, the shins. The shin bone makes an ideal kicking surface, yet the many nerve endings in the lower leg make it an acutely sensitive part of the body. Elite Thai forces, and some Korean units, use the technique of the Thai boxer to condition the shins – a fairly brutal method of kicking a bamboo post repeatedly until the nerves are deadened and calcification of the area builds up a hardened kicking surface. Other shin conditioning exercises include rubbing a hard stick or bottle up and down the shin bone until the desired strength is achieved, not for the faint hearted. These may seem like extreme methods of training, however, in a combat situation this level of conditioning can make an enormous difference to the trained soldier, the ability to endure a certain level of pain is crucial.

CHAPTER 8

Chokes and Headlocks

There is no real set situation where a choke or headlock is used. It is just a case, when grappling, of constantly looking for appropriate openings for these formidable methods. If employed correctly, they can be brilliant stopping techniques.

I f an enemy soldier cannot be neutralised with punches or kicks, it may be necessary to grab or spin him into a sucker punch, choke, strangle, bear hug, headlock or other close-range attack. At grabbing range, other parts of the body besides hand and feet become natural weapons – elbows and shoulders, knees and hips, even the head – but the chokes and headlocks that he can apply with his hands and arms offer the soldier some of his best opportunities for subduing his opponent.

Devastatingly effective if employed correctly, they are brilliant stopping techniques and can render an opponent unconscious instantly. The beauty of these techniques is that they are not a complex skill and can be used from a variety of angles. Some of the strangles use the attacker's clothing as an aid for leverage, while others, like the naked strangle locks, do not. Many may be executed while in the vertical position and others are more effective in the horizontal, ground-work position. When mastery with headlocks and chokes is achieved, it is possible to flow

LEFT: Wrist and arm locks are important techniques for the soldier to master. There is no real right or wrong way of getting to grips with chokes and locks – it is a question of overcoming your opponent.

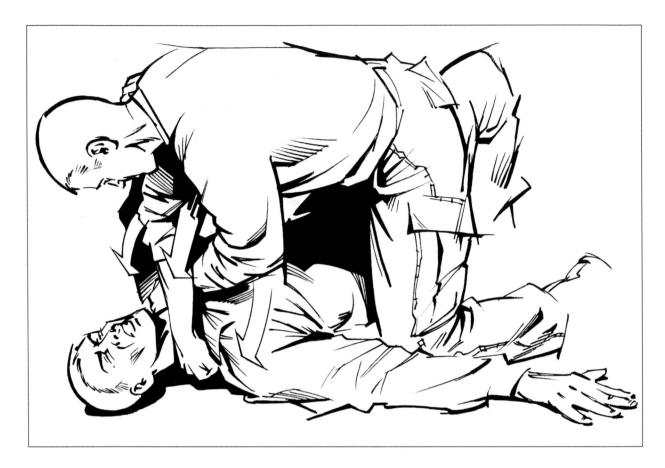

ABOVE: For the scissors choke, the soldier sits on top of and astride the opponent and crosses his hands with palms down and grabs the opponent's lapels as deeply to the back of the neck as possible. He applies pressure to his neck by pushing both elbows downwards and forcing both wrists into either side of his neck.

from one version to another, improvising. The technique is not important, stopping the attacker is.

Fundamentally, the purpose of the choke or headlock is to cut off the blood supply to the attacker's brain. Chokes and headlocks stop the oxygen supply by compressing the jugular and carotid veins. A choke can also cut off the oxygen supply by compressing the windpipe. Using these methods can induce unconsciousness within seconds and in practising the chokes and locks extreme caution is always exercised, because a mistake can prove fatal. When a choke, lock or hold is applied, the opponent taps the floor, himself, his partner or anything close enough to tap to signal submission. The tap system is employed at all times and a choke is always released immediately if the practice partner taps.

ATTACKING WITH THE HANDS AT CLOSE QUARTERS

Hands can be used to pull and twist while in grappling distance; to palm - heel or gouge with the fingers extended. There are no better instruments to use as attacking tools than the hands, whether punching, poking or grabbing. Hands are the most accessible weapons on the human anatomy.

Here are some of the ways a soldier uses them to choke an opponent. The claw squeeze is simple and highly effective, especially if the opponent and the soldier are grappling on the floor – the soldier grips the opponent's larynx, which is situated at the top of the windpipe just below the chin, and squeezes tightly. In the scissors choke a soldier sitting on top of and astride his opponent crosses his hands with palms down and grabs the opponent's lapels as deeply to the back of the neck as possible. He applies pressure to the opponent's neck by pushing both elbows simultaneously downwards forcing both wrists into either side of the neck. In the scarf hold and fist choke a soldier sitting at his opponent's right side places his right arm around his opponent's neck, taking a firm grip on the opponent's clothes with his right hand. He wraps the opponent's left arm firmly around his own waist and holds his sleeve with his left hand. The soldier clamps his left arm over his opponent's right arm firmly. Keeping his right knee bent and close to his opponent's right shoulder, the opponent is firmly held down. The soldier makes a fist with his left hand and pushes it hard into the right side of his throat. The technique for choking with the collar from the front is to grab the opponent's collar on each side with a cross-hand hold. The soldier twists his clenched hands inward, using the thumb knuckles to press hard against the opponent's neck for strangulation.

ATTACKING WITH THE ARMS AT CLOSE QUARTERS

The shoulders can be effective for close-in fighting, if thrust into an opponent's windpipe or face. However, a

BELOW: When the soldier makes a fist choke he places his right arm around his opponent's neck taking a firm grip on his clothes with his right hand. Keeping the opponent pinned down, the soldier makes a fist with his left hand and pushes it hard into the right side of his throat.

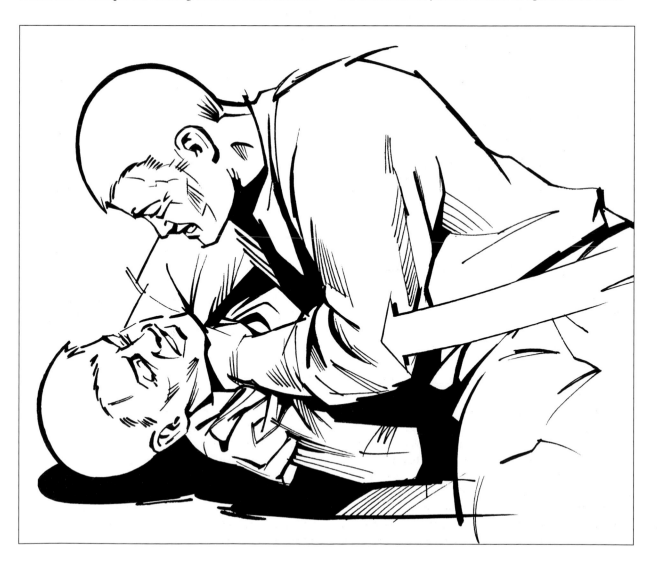

grappling soldier is likely to strike more close-quarters blows with his elbows. And the opportunities he will be looking for most alertly – and manoeuvring to create – are those that will allow him to apply his forearms in powerful chokes and holds.

The soldier can choke with the forearm if the opponent is pinned on the ground. The soldier seizes the opponent's collar and presses down heavily on the opponent's throat with his forearm, simultaneously pressing him to the ground with his side and not letting him loose. In the forearm upward choke, choking is done with an arm around the throat applying a quick, upward pressure, squeezing or twisting the head left and right.

In the side headlock, a soldier places his right arm around his opponent's neck and hugs the opponent's head tightly into the side of his own body. The palm of the soldier's right fist faces inward so that the bony part of his right wrist is into the opponent's neck. He places his left palm heel underneath his right fist and applies pressure on the neck and jugular, pushing up with the left hand and squeezing in with the right arm hand.

An armlock is one of the best come-alongs. Properly

BELOW: Choking with the collar from the front begins simply by gripping the opponent's collar firmly on both sides (A). This can be an effective method of close-quarter attacking.

RIGHT: The soldier then pulls one side of the collar across the throat and up, pulling the other side in the opposite direction to make a wringing stranglehold (B).

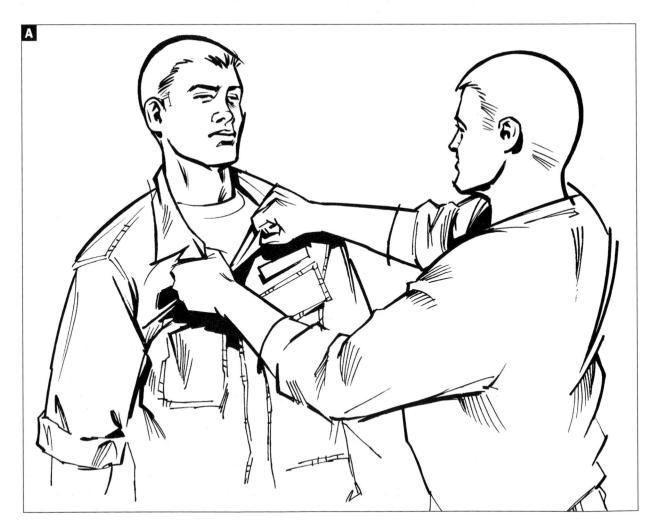

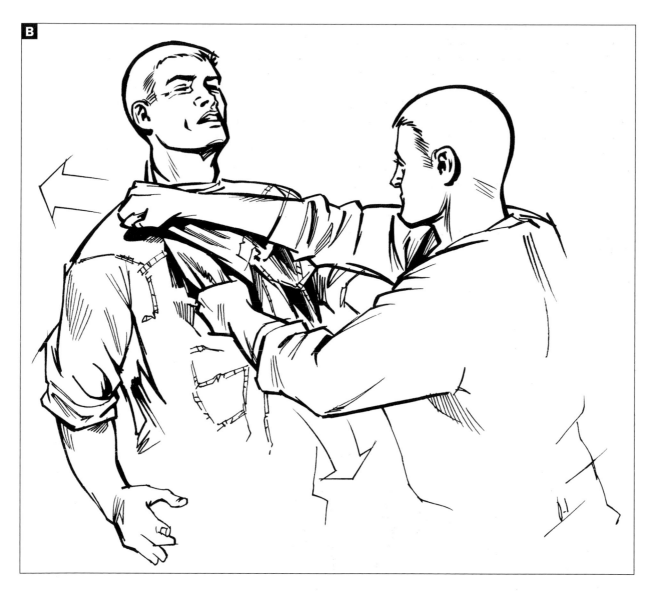

applied, this lock makes a hold sufficiently strong for escorting a prisoner a short distance. It gives the soldier control of his opponent completely if pressure is maintained on the forearm and it is very useful as a compliance hold or in taking a man to the ground before tying him up. A speedy application of an armlock can constitute an attack, but it is easier applied as a mastering hold after the enemy has been subdued by some other means.

FOREARM CHOKES AND LOCKS FROM BEHIND

As a basic technique for attacking the enemy from behind, the soldier wraps his right arm around the opponent's neck, with his elbow snugly under the opponent's chin. The soldier puts his upper left arm on the opponent's left shoulder and lays the straightened fingers of his right hand in the crook of his left elbow. Then the soldier puts his left forearm and hand to the back of the opponent's head or nape of his neck and chokes by squeezing his arms towards each other.

In the sitting neck-break the opponent is sitting on a chair and the soldier approaches him from the rear. He reaches across and under the opponent's chin, with his hand

coming around to the back of the opponent's neck. From this position, the locking of the arm plus an upward and backward jerk will cause the neck to break immediately.

In the reverse naked choke, a soldier standing behind his opponent throws his right arm around and across the opponent's throat. He clasps his right hand with his left and applies pressure to the throat by pulling backwards with the combined force of both hands. For maximum effect he makes sure that the bony part of his right wrist is against the throat as opposed to the softer forearm. He also tries to pull the opponent backwards and off his feet. This lessens the opponent's chances of fighting back.

In the sliding reverse collar-lock, a soldier standing behind his opponent places his right arm around the opponent's throat and grips hold of his jacket or shirt. He then places his left arm under his opponent's left armpit and seizes the right side of his clothes before applying pressure by choking in a wringing motion.

In the upper throat lift, the soldier takes the opponent's head under his right armpit and slides his right arm under and across his throat. The soldier's right fist palm is facing into his own body to ensure that the bony part of his wrist is along the opponent's throat. The soldier places his left

palm heel under his right fist. He applies pressure on the opponent's throat by pushing the right arm up and into the throat with the left hand while at the same time pulling the right arm into the throat.

A LEAPING STRANGLE
When wiping out a sentry by an attack from the rear without weapons, the first principle to observe is that the approach must be a noiseless one. The attack may be launched from a leap over the remaining metre or so, because many people under attack in this situation have a highly developed animal instinct which gives them warning of a hostile presence, although they do not see or hear anything.

The sentry has to be strangled quickly and silently. As the soldier leaps, his fist drives into the sentry's right kidney with enough force that the man will bend backwards and come off-balance. At the same time, the soldier's left forearm swings around the sentry's neck. These two blows are enough initially to stun the sentry for the few vital seconds necessary to apply a strangle hold.

From this position, with his left arm across the sentry's

BELOW: The soldier chokes with the forearm after pinning the opponent down on the ground and seizing his collar and pressing down heavily on his throat.

ABOVE: An underarm upwards choke is done with an arm around the throat and quick, upward pressure is applied as well as squeezing or twisting the head to the left and right. The best way to escape from a frontal attack is to respond by grabbing the enemy's testicles.

neck, the soldier places his right hand on the back of the sentry's head and hooks his left hand inside the bend in the elbow of the sentry's right arm. In this position, the soldier exerts enormous leverage by pushing forwards with his right hand and pulling back with his left at the same time.

In moments, the sentry is strangled or his neck broken. The soldier makes sure during this hold that he is continu-

ally pulling his victim backwards so that he is off-balance. This is even more vital if the soldier is shorter than the sentry. In this case, the use of the knee instead of the fist is the best for the first blow.

FRONTAL HEADLOCK

A strangle hold may also be applied from the front. This lock is easier when the opponent's head happens to be lowered, as it would be if he was attempting to make a grab for a soldier's legs or waist. If standing, the soldier swings his right arm forward and around bringing the palm of the hand against the back of the enemy's neck. By giving his

ASSASSINATION

The arts of assassination are mainly the province of the world's elite special forces, and consequently they receive more lethally directed unarmed combat training than regular military units. This repetoire can be truly frightening. During his time serving with the SAS, Charles Beckwith (who went on to found the US Delta unit) acquired 86 different methods of killing with the bare hands. Other units, such as the Israeli Special Forces and the US Green Berets, have similar deadly skills. Assassination techniques are mostly geared towards the silent removal of enemy personnel, especially sentries on guard or terrorists in hostage-taking situations. RM Commandos and the SBS (Special Boat Service) during WWII, for instance, were taught powerful strangulation techniques for use on sentries during amphibious operations against enemy coastal emplacements where stealth and concealment were vital. Strangulation is indeed the primary unarmed assassination technique. If correctly applied, unconsciousness results in only a few seconds and, if the lock is maintained, death shortly after. Such techniques also have the virtue of cutting off the recipient's ability to shout or speak. This forced silence was invaluable to US Navy SEAL units operating in Vietnam between 1965 and 1973. Often sent deep into Viet Cong territory on surveillance and killing missions, they noiselessly disposed of many VC personnel using either knives, garrotes or their bare hands before disappearing back into the jungle without alerting the enemy. Today, elite units like the SEALs closely guard their lethal range of unarmed skills and make every effort to restrict public access to their killing techniques.

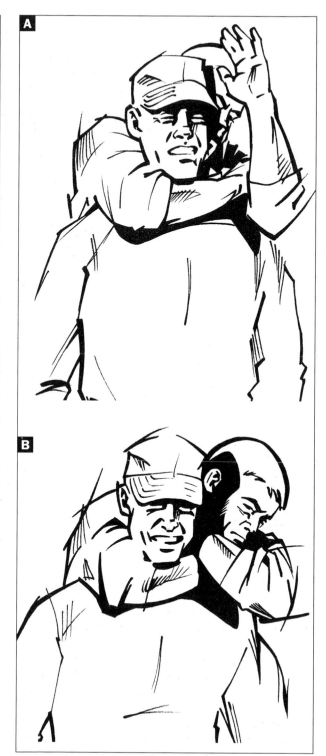

RIGHT: Choking using forearms. The special forces soldier wraps the right arm around the neck, with the elbow under the chin. The soldier puts his upper left arm on the opponent's left shoulder and lays the straightened fingers of his right hand in the crook of his left elbow (A). Then the soldier puts his left forearm and hand to the back of the enemy's head and chokes by squeezing his arms towards each other (B).

body weight to the swing, the soldier will cause the enemy to bring his head forward and downward to a position where the soldier's left arm can be brought up and under the enemy's throat and locked around his neck, with the soldier's right hand taking a firm grip on his left as reinforcement. When the opponent is in that position, the soldier can move to the final phase, causing strangulation or a neck-break by pushing his hips forwards and shoulders well back, lifting upward as he does so.

ATTACKING WITH ELBOWS

As any dirty footballer can explain, the elbows are effective from any angle in close range. They are almost as versatile as the hands, though usually used from a shorter range. Because of their close proximity to the body

BELOW AND RIGHT: Leaping strangle. When wiping out a sentry by an attack from the rear, without weapons, the first principle to observe is that the approach must be silent (A). The attack should be launched from a leap over the remaining metre or so (B).

they are potentially more powerful than the hands. However, they lack the feel, accuracy and cunning of the hands. They may be used off the front leg or rear to uppercut, thrust sideways or, while grappling in range, in a downward strike.

The elbows are just a shortened version of the hands.

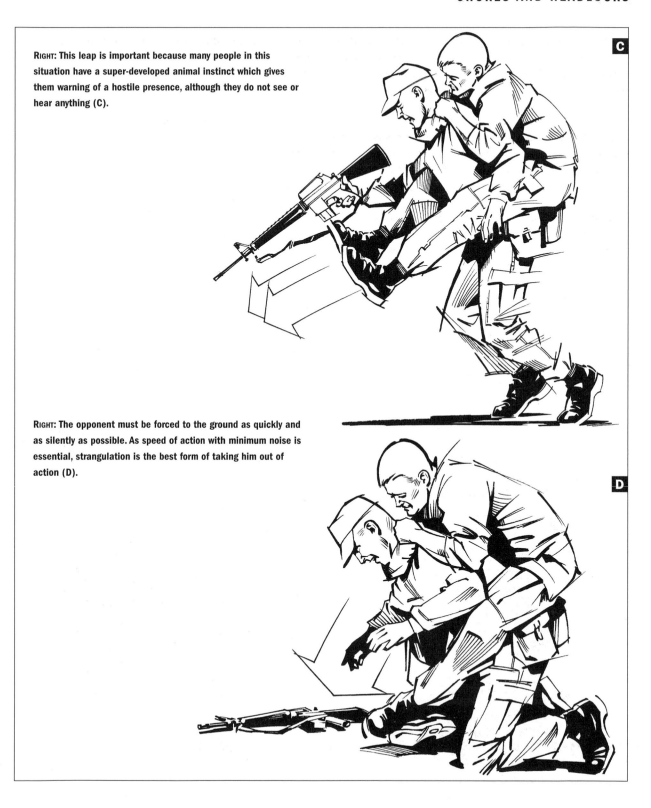

RIGHT: This leap is important because many people in this situation have a super-developed animal instinct which gives them warning of a hostile presence, although they do not see or hear anything (C).

RIGHT: The opponent must be forced to the ground as quickly and as silently as possible. As speed of action with minimum noise is essential, strangulation is the best form of taking him out of action (D).

C

D

They are only used as back-up to hand techniques or when it is not possible or practical (because the fighting is at such close quarters) to punch. The technique for hooking and uppercutting with the point of the elbow from front or rear is the same principle as for using the fist.

A downwards strike with the elbow can be used against a waist or leg grab. The soldier lifts the striking arm up high with the palm of the hand facing away from himself and pulls it down with a rapid descent, aiming the point of the elbow at the spine, neck or rib cage.

A side thrust is good against an assailant attacking from the side. The soldier brings the striking arm across the front

ABOVE: An elbow strike may be used off the front or rear leg to uppercut, thrust sideways or whilst grappling in range as a downward strike. In essence, the elbows are a shortened version of the hands, used as back-up to hand techniques or when it is not possible or practical to punch.

of his chest, palm inwards, as far as it will go, then thrusts back along the same route, aiming the point of the elbow into the oncoming or stationary attacker. The best targets are the solar plexus, throat or face.

A reverse elbow strike against an opponent behind starts with the soldier stretching his striking arm out ahead of

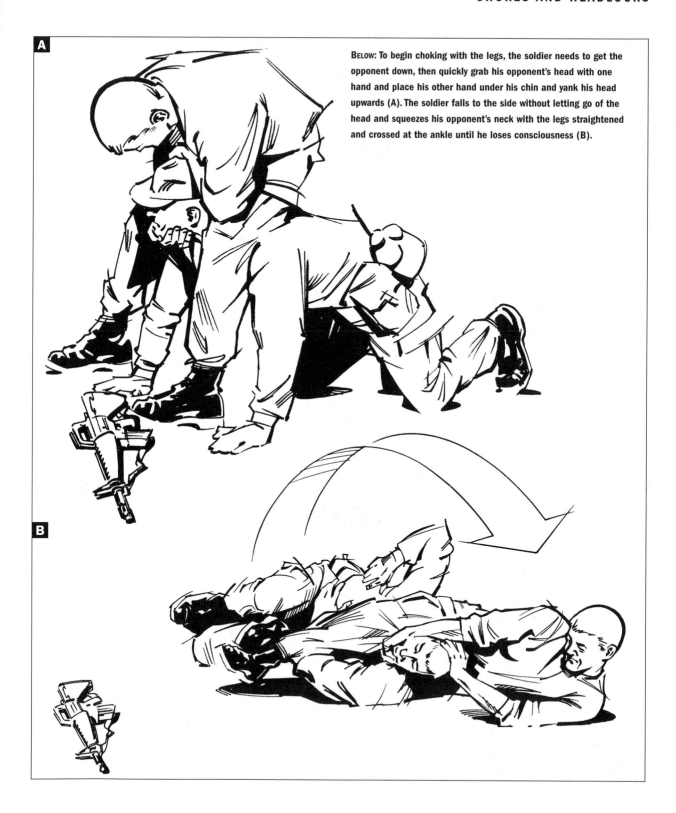

A

BELOW: To begin choking with the legs, the soldier needs to get the opponent down, then quickly grab his opponent's head with one hand and place his other hand under his chin and yank his head upwards (A). The soldier falls to the side without letting go of the head and squeezes his opponent's neck with the legs straightened and crossed at the ankle until he loses consciousness (B).

B

KRAV MAGA AND THE ISRAELI DEFENCE FORCE

Krav Maga is the Israeli Defence Force's unique and purpose-developed unarmed combat system. Taught to every IDF recruit, the Israeli Police and Security Services and also US law enforcement agencies, Krav Maga is a pure self-defence form. It instructs in viable, dangerous and instinctive techniques for dealing with almost every unarmed combat situation a soldier could encounter, from dealing with a single opponent armed with a knife to defending against multiple assailants. Krav Maga's intense practicality and real value as a military self-defence form is in the main due to the background of its founder, Imi Lichtenfeld. Lichtenfeld was born in 1910 in Czechoslovakia, his father being a circus acrobat, wrestler and, later, a Chief Detective Inspector in the police. The young Lichentfeld inherited his father's passion for combat sports and he took up wrestling and boxing with real competitive success. However, with the spread of fascism preceding WWII Lichtenfeld found himself engaged in the realities of street fighting, often in the defence of Jews against gangs of fascist youths. He thus came to understand intimately the nature of actual combat as opposed to competitive combat, and it was this knowledge he took with him to Israel when he emigrated there in 1942.

Once in Israel, Lichtenfeld joined the Haganah (the precursor to the IDF) and was put to task instructing new recruits in unarmed combat. Because the Israeli state was born into war from the very day it was formed, Lichtenfeld had to transfer totally serious skills to a very mixed bag of soldiers of various ages and fitness levels. Krav Maga was the result. Because combat was a real and pressing possibility for IDF recruits, Krav Maga had nothing extraneous in its training programme and quickly gave an individual a practical body of unarmed combat skills through a compact and realistic period of instruction. Lichtenfeld went on to become chief instructor for the Military School for Physical Training and Krav Maga of the IDF, a position he held for over 20 years. From the humblest infantryman to Israel's battle-tested special forces, all IDF soldiers benefit from Krav Maga training. Without a competitive or sporting element, Krav Maga is perhaps the purest self-defence form in the world.

himself. He then sharply brings it back, aiming the point of his elbow at the assailant, simultaneously stepping back to add weight to the attack. Best targets are the solar plexus, throat or face.

ATTACKING WITH THE LEGS

The hip is pivotal in throwing techniques, to which we will return. If thrust into the opponent's mid-section, it ensures depth to the throw and unbalances him before the throw. And the legs can be used for choking. As soon as the opponent is down, the soldier quickly grabs him by the hair with one hand and places his other hand under his chin and yanks his head upwards. The soldier falls to the side without letting go of his head and squeezes his neck using the legs straightened and crossed at the ankle until he loses consciousness.

Knees may be used to thrust inward, upward and around towards targets as low as the opponent's knee or high as his head. Knee-first drops onto the felled opponent are used as a fearsome finishing weapon. This technique was made famous by ferocious Thai boxers who used their knees as naturally and as effectively as the Western boxer uses his hands. The knees are relegated to fighting at close quarters, though they are irreplaceable when applicable. They are a very basic and very accessible weapon, whose effective use in many circumstances does not require a great deal of skill.

The upward knee strike to the groin or testicles is a simple but effective technique. The knee is lifted upwards as sharply as possible because a slow push movement would be ineffective. The quicker the ascent, the greater the impact. If applying the same technique to the opponent's face or head, it is customary first to grab his head by the hair or ears or by coupling the fingers of both hands at the back of his skull and pulling his head down rapidly towards the knee. Simultaneously, the attacking knee is brought upwards to meet the descending target. As they meet, the head is smashed onto the knee.

The forward knee technique uses the knee as the attacking tool, instead of the foot, in much the same way as the thrusting front kick. It relies heavily on the grip the attacker has on his opponent. The move starts by grabbing the opponent's clothing tightly at about shoulder level and aggressively pulling the opponent's body towarda your knee. At the same time, the attacking knee thrusts forward to meet the opponent's body on its descent.

The round-house knee technique is much the same as

the roundhouse kick. It uses the knee as the attacking tool instead of the foot. It is also relegated to grappling distance and relies heavily on the pulling and grabbing support of the soldier's hands. It may be used very effectively to attack the opponent's knee, thigh or body. An advanced exponent may even attack the head.

The attacking knee is lifted up and slightly away from the soldier's body then thrust towards the opponent's knee, thigh or body. At the same time the opponent's clothing is pulled towards the attacking knee. On impact the technique is to thrust your hips forward behind your full body weight.

The knee drop is a very damaging technique to finish off an opponent who is already lying on the floor. Logically, the heavier the attacker is the more effective this technique will be, although it doesn't rely entirely on body weight for its effectiveness. It can be dangerous for the attacker attempting the knee drop, because of the danger of being pulled into grappling range by the opponent on the floor.

It involves dropping all the weight forward and down onto the opponent, landing on the target area of ribs or

head with the point of the attacking knee. For added effect, exponents sometimes jump up so that they are landing on the opponent from a greater height. But they only do that if they are sure that their opponent is past resistance.

ATTACKING WITH THE HEAD

The head can become a weapon at close distance. It may be used to butt from the right, from the left, from the front or to the rear, using the corner, front or rear surface.

The forward head butt is a great way of starting an attack. The soldier lurches his body forward followed by the front of his head, whiplashing it into an opponent's nose, eyes or jaw. He takes care not to hit the opponent's teeth. Although a blow in the teeth is very painful for the recipient, teeth are potentially very dangerous to the

BELOW: An upwards knee to the groin or testicles is a simple but effective technique. Grab your opponent around the neck if possible and lift the knee upwards as sharply as possible – a slow push movement would be ineffective as the technique relies on impact.

ABOVE: The forward head butt is an effective way of starting an attack. Lurch the body forward followed by the front of the head, whiplashing it onto an opponent's nose, eyes or jaw. Care should be taken not to hit his teeth.

RIGHT ABOVE AND BELOW: The upward head butt is also effective if executed in an upward manner using the crown to attack. It is most effectively employed from within grappling range when the forehead is in the region of the opponent's chest.

attacker. If a head-butting soldier is gripping his opponent's clothes at the time of the head butt, he should pull them rapidly towards him to increase the impact of the head butt.

The head butt is also effective if executed in an upward manner using the crown to attack. The upward head butt is generally employed from within grappling range when the attacker's forehead is in the region of his opponent's chest.

All head attacks are from close range and can be employed with or without the support of a soldier's hands to pull. Power in the head butt relies on two things; the whiplash effect and the propelling body weight.

ABOVE AND LEFT: Biting is only effective within wrestling distance, and any protruding parts of the anatomy can be bitten, including the nose and ears. Many find the thought of biting an adversary off-putting, but when a person is being attacked, it loses its repugnance.

Spitting into an opponent's face or eyes can be a great distracting factor that may lead a soldier onto a better grip or attack. Teeth are effective within wrestling distance. Anything can be bitten, especially protruding parts of the anatomy such as the nose, lips and ears. When a soldier is being attacked and his life is threatened, it becomes natural. The soldier attacks fiercely and gets as strong a bite and grip as possible. In these circumstances, he is very wary of a 'plea bargaining' opponent who will offer anything to be freed from the bite. The ploy is often to feign capitulation then, as soon as he is released he continues his attack with added ferocity.

Breaking Free

A trained soldier will fight to resist being grabbed into grappling range, and if he does happen to be held there by an opponent he will fight to break the hold.

Resisting being grabbed by an opponent is an absolute priority for a soldier. He will, of course, make any defensive move the first element in a strategy to counter-attack. Part and parcel of breaking free, it will always be the soldier's aim to stun or disable the opponent if he can, then move directly to a takedown, finishing the opponent on the ground.

Much of the soldier's training will have consisted of fighting with partners to try out strategies for grabbing and breaking free. One method is for a soldier to go in the centre of a sand pit and another one attack him using a grab, first from behind and then from the side, without being told what specific grab to use. This results in him making a natural selection of grabs, which makes the attack realistic. After several days of this kind of practice, the many attack possibilities are narrowed down through the soldiers' choices to those that an attacker is most likely to use.

The training for countering grab attacks often includes significant amounts of practice in an environment very similar to that in which soldiers will be operating. This includes night fighting and amidst obstacles. Training may occur in a dark building or among trees where the only possible attacking technique is some sort of grab. The instructor will sometimes make the trainees fight in strange, confined areas. For example, he may borrow a bus and set up fights among the tight seats and in the narrow aisle.

LEFT: Part of the training of a US Marine Security Guard's duty is to disarm a potential assailant.

121

BODY WEAPONS FOR RESISTING GRABS AND HOLDS

At close quarters a soldier will use his teeth to bite, or use his fingers for an eye gouge or lip tear, both as a means of breaking the opponent's hold and of weakening him for a counter-attack. The eye gouge is accomplished by placing a thumb on the inside of the eye socket next to the nose and flicking the eyeball out toward the edge of the cheek. For a lip tear, the soldier hooks his thumb in the corner of the opponent's mouth and tears toward the hinge of the jaw. However, these techniques are not sufficient to put a man permanently out of action, once his fighting instincts are aroused.

Escape techniques of choking, twisting and hitting are the primary means of successfully breaking free and performing counter-attacks. The most dynamic technique is the blow, used to escape restraints, grasps and holds. Using the elbow against the stomach or other tender parts of the anatomy is always good for breaking a hold, and

very effective, as well as such other strategies as stamping on the instep, kicking the shins, pulling hair and breaking fingers. One or a combination of these is sufficient to release almost any hold, such as a grappling hold from the rear or the front, or a standing front chokehold. Any choke-hold can be broken if one of the fingers is grabbed and broken.

Sometimes the technique is simply to grab back whatever the assailant is holding. To escape an arm grip the soldier bends his legs to lower his centre of gravity and to make it easier to break his enemy's grip, then pulls his arm toward himself to break free. He finishes the move with a punch to the opponent's stomach.

DEFENCES FOR ATTACKS FROM THE FRONT

Blows against an opponent attacking from the front can be delivered with fingers in the eyes – usually the index and middle – with a short jab quickly withdrawn and followed

BELOW: The soldier escapes from an arm grip by first bending his legs to lower his centre of gravity (A). To make it easier to break his enemy's grip, he pulls his arm sharply towards himself (B). He finishes the move with a side-armed smash to the stomach (C).

RIGHT: Escaping from a body hold from the front can be extremely tricky (A). One method is to push the attacker's head sharply backwards from underneath his chin (B). If enough force is exerted the attacker will fall backwards (C).

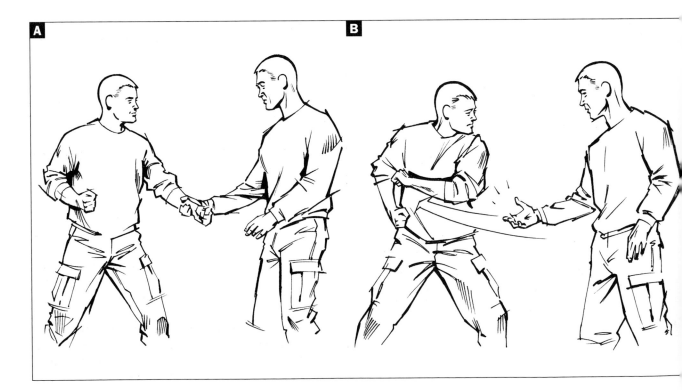

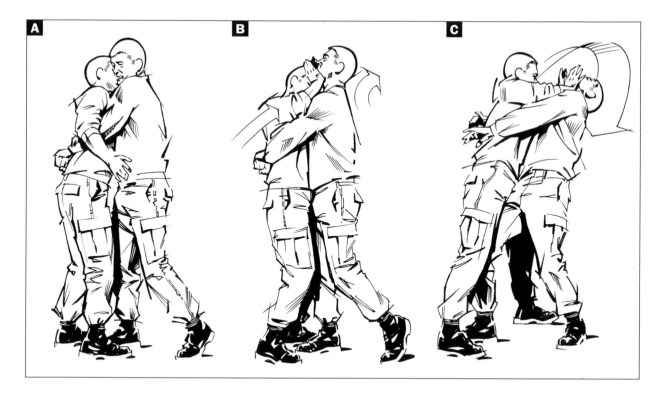

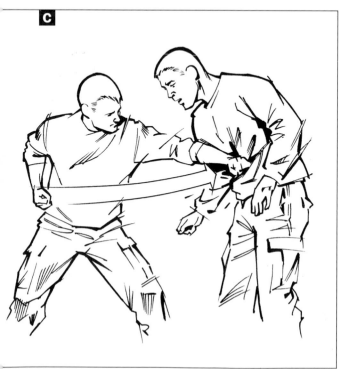

up with a more damaging attack, or a head butt in the face or nose if the opponent has the soldier by the arms, shoulders or belt. Other possibilities are to hit up under the nose or ears, or hit the lower lip or the muscles at the side of the neck. Kicks to vulnerable points are often used in escaping from frontal attacks. They include kicking and kneeing the groin slamming the opponent's face onto your knee and head butting his face.

Against an attack at the legs from the front, counter-attacks include:

- throws over the back,
- knees to the face and chest and an elbow in the back between the shoulder blades against the vertebrae (this is usually very effective),
- clamping the head for choking, with an arm around the throat and a quick, upward pressure and squeezing or twisting of the opponent's head to the side.

Other techniques in escaping restraints from the front include: hand and arm blows using the fist, edge of hand, or elbow, swung from below into the stomach, neck or face. A straight left jab to the opponent's face might be the

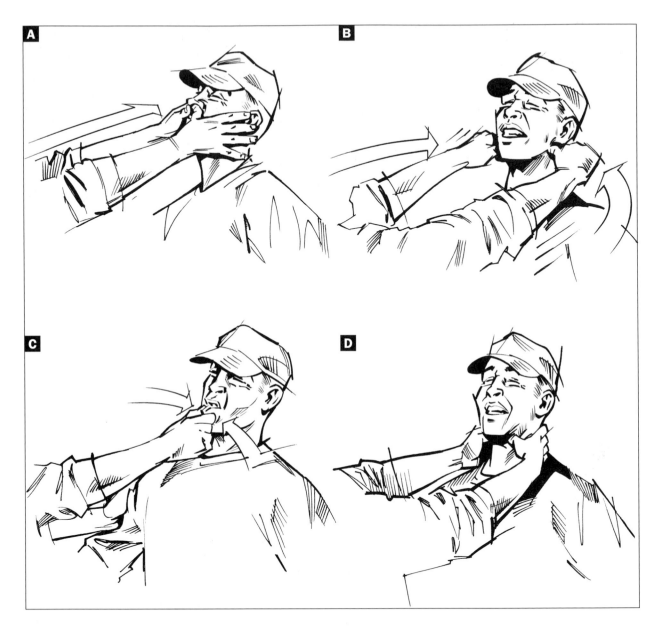

ABOVE: Hitting up under the nose is a simple but painful attack (A). Thumb blows to the base of the ears is another useful method (B). The lower lip is an easy and sensitive target (C). Attacking the muscles at the side of the neck can mobilise an opponent (D).

only blow needed to set the soldier up for a vicious counter-attack to another part of the opponent's body.

Another way of escaping from a frontal attack is to grab the assailant's testicles (assuming the opponent is a man!).

This requires forceful grasping and twisting back and forth and trying to pull his attacker toward him. Simple, but if done well it is very effective.

To escape from a body hold from the front, a soldier starts with a head butt into his attacker's face or strikes him under the chin or nose with the heel of his hand. He follows up with a knee to the groin or a shove under the chin. Once the attacker is on the ground, the soldier uses a wrap-up kick to a vulnerable spot.

To counter a bear hug from the front, a soldier uses his hands on the opponent's face to attack the chin, nose and eyes. Once he forces the opponent to back away, he trips him and hits him as hard as he can. If the soldier falls down or goes to ground, he makes sure that he keeps facing the opponent as he approaches. He gathers himself and if he is on his back, meets the opponent with heel kicks to the shins or knees. The soldier uses the soles and heels of his boots to ward off the opponent's kicks, but is aware that staying down too long is dangerous, if he is wearing hob-nail boots this can be particularly effective. If a soldier falls down, he tries to get off his back onto all fours, then off his knees to an upright stance. In getting up, the soldier may have to throw himself at his attacker, but it may be better to back off.

ABOVE: Marine Security Guards here practise compliance neck holds, drawing the head back from under the chin and anchoring it against the chest.

WRISTLOCKS

If applied with force, attacks on the joints allow a soldier to break holds and chokes, they can be very effective when in a difficult situation. The wristlock is a joint manipulation technique used to control the opponent and cause damage to the wrist. To execute the wristlock the soldier:

- reaches over the opponent's arm and quickly grasps his hand,
- places his thumb in the middle of the back of the opponent's hand,

ABOVE: An elbow in the back between the shoulder blades against the vertebrae can stop an opponent dramatically. This method is best deployed as swiftly and as hard as possible, a soldier needs to be able to time this move well.

RIGHT: Other techniques for escaping restraints from the front include: an elbow swung roundhouse-fashion into the face (A); a violent elbow uppercut to the chin (B); a straight elbow jab to the face (C); and a heavy hammerfist blow down onto the bridge of the nose (D).

- wraps his fingers around the opponent's hand beneath his thumb,
- turns his hand forcefully upwards until the palm is vertical to the ground,
- grasps his opponent's hand with his free hand, places the opponent's thumbs together and wraps his fingers around the hand beneath the little finger to provide added leverage,
- then pushes the opponent's hand at an angle to the out-side of the elbow and pushes him downwards until he is on the ground,
- then uses his knee to lock the opponent's fully extended elbow while maintaining pressure to the wristlock (this maintains control of the opponent).

During unarmed combat training, the soldier applies the wristlock with consistent pressure. During combat, he applies the wristlock with a forceful snapping motion. It is important for a soldier to learn the distinction in training.

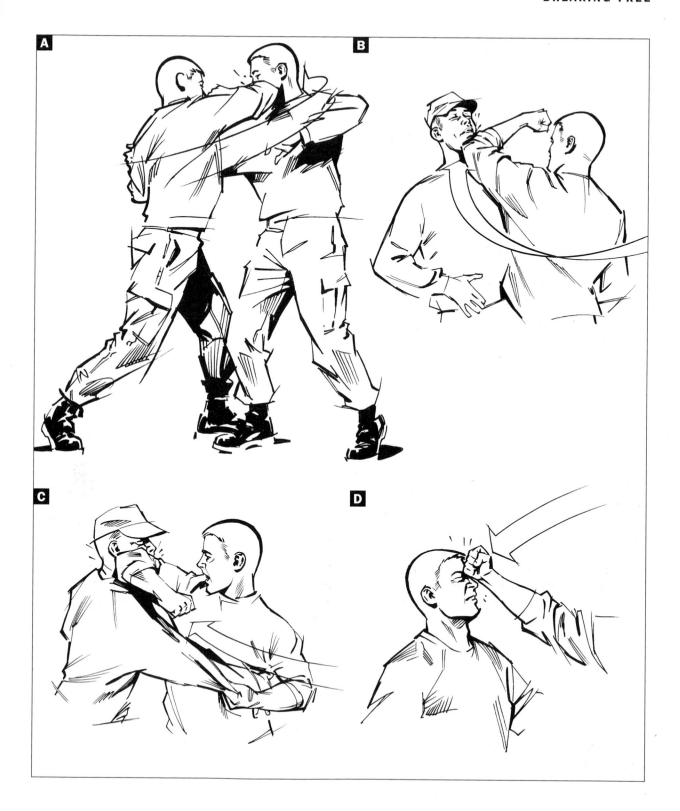

REVERSE WRISTLOCK

In the reverse wristlock, the soldier:

- reaches over the opponent's arms and quickly grasps his hand,
- places his thumb in the middle of the back of the opponent's hand,
- wraps his fingers around his hand beneath his little finger,
- then turns his hand forcefully to the inside with his palm vertical to the ground,
- grasps the opponent's hand with his free hand and places the opponent's thumbs together and wraps his fingers around his hand beneath his little finger to

BELOW: To escape from a headlock the soldier should first pull down heavily on the choking arm to relieve pressure (A) and follow up with one of two options: either grasp and crush the opponent's testicles (B) or perform a hammerfist blow to the same region (C).

provide added leverage,

- applies pressure while driving his hand forcefully towards his shoulder,
- pushes downwards until the opponent is on the ground,
- uses his knee to lock the opponent's fully extended elbow while maintaining pressure to the wristlock (this maintains control of the opponent).

WRIST RELEASE

This is an invaluable method when an enemy has grasped the soldier by one or both arms. Probably, one of the first things an opponent will do in a fight is to grab the soldier either by the wrist or the forearm because he wants to protect himself as well as immobilise the soldier's attack.

When the opponent grasps the soldier by the wrist, regardless of how strong he is, his thumb, which is the weak side of his grip, will not be stronger than the soldier's entire arm. By a twist of the wrist outward against the

thumb, the soldier can break the hold with a sudden jerk. The entire movement has to be swift. The soldier always twists his wrist against the opponent's thumb, regardless of whether it is his weaker or stronger hand, and this is enough to break the grip.

If the enemy grabs the soldier's wrist with both hands, by jerking upward toward the thumbs, the same release can be effected with a little more effort.

DEFENCE FOR A SIDE HEADLOCK

If the opponent attempts a side headlock, the soldier brutally delivers a right hand groin strike to loosen the hold. To defend against the side headlock:

- he uses the palm of his right hand to strike the opponent's groin,
- grabs, squeezes and twists the opponent's testicles forcefully,
- grabs the opponent's right wrist with his left hand,

ABOVE: The correct execution of a front jab. The front shoulder is pushed into the punch to add body weight and the punch is placed accurately on the jawline. The other fist is prepared for the follow-up.

- steps under the opponent's arm as the hold loosens,
- delivers a powerful right forearm strike to the opponent's extended elbow (this damages his elbow and drives the opponent's upper body down),
- maintain control of the opponent's arm and applies pressure to his injured elbow,
- executes a rear leg front kick to the opponent's face,
- grabs the opponent behind the neck, rotates his hips and executes a leg sweep taking the opponent to the ground,
- executes a heel stomp swiftly and violently to the opponent's head as a finishing technique.

BREAKING A FRONT CHOKEHOLD

If the opponent is trying to choke him, the soldier must loosen the opponent's grip on his throat or neck and then be ready with a counter-attack. One way for the soldier to break free is to twist the attacker's thumb. Another simple way of getting out of a chokehold from the front is for the soldier to place his hands between the attacker's arms and smash them apart to break the hold. Or the soldier seizes the attacker's hands then bends forward to make him loosen his grip. As he breaks free of the hold, he smashes his elbow into the side of the opponent's neck or delivers a blow to his face.

Alternatively, to break free the soldier can forcefully deliver forearm strikes to the opponent's right arm to permanantly damage the elbow. To defend against the front choke, he:

- strikes the opponent's inside right wrist with his right forearm while striking the outside of the opponent's

BELOW: A hold on the wrist is easily broken by attacking the individual digits that make up the grip rather than the hand as a whole. The outside digits (thumb and little finger) are the most vulnerable and can be prized away from the grip, snapped back and broken.

RIGHT: Escaping a choke from behind involves the soldier dropping to one knee (A). Using the momentum of his body weight the opponent is thrown forward. The effect of landing so heavily and unexpectedly makes him an easy captive (B).

right elbow with his left forearm,

- steps back quickly with his right foot while maintaining pressure to the damaged elbow,
- grabs the opponent's wrist with his right hand and drives his left forearm into the injured elbow causing the opponent to bend at the waist,
- executes a rear leg front kick to the opponent's face,
- switches grips quickly by grabbing the opponent by the

BELOW: A chokehold escape. The soldier makes as much space as he can (A) and then violently swings his right arm over the attacker's arm in a up-and-over punching style (B). This breaks the hold and allows the soldier to drive his elbow straight back into the attacker's face.

A

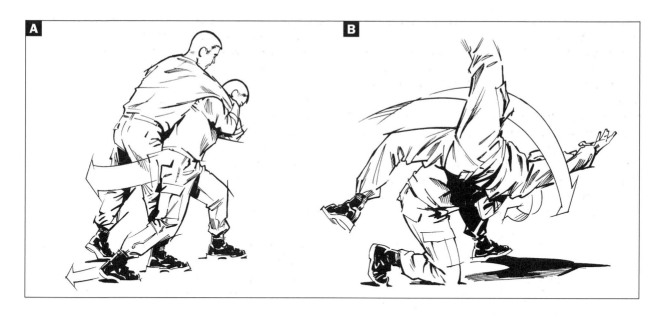

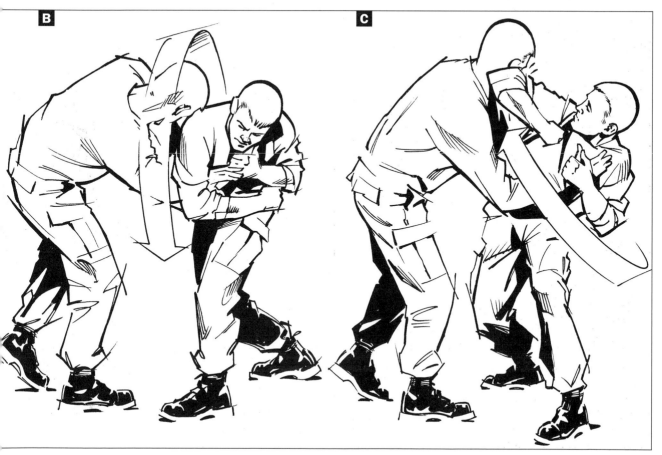

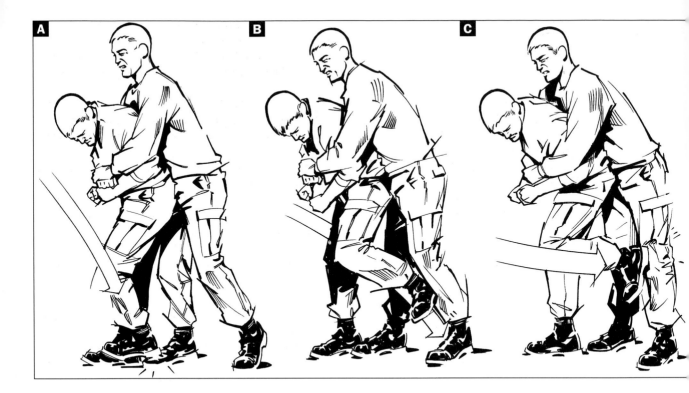

ABOVE: To escape from a bear hug from behind is difficult but not entirely impossible. Stamping on the enemy's toe with heavy boots is a good start (A). Back heeling into the shin is another painful way of getting the attacker's grip loosened (B). Smashing the sole of a boot into a knee is guaranteed to hurt the attacker (C). If there is room to manouevre, a sharp backward kick into the groin will have an instant effect (D).

back of the neck with his right hand and grabbing the opponent's wrist with his left hand,

● maintains control and body contact with the opponent while changing grips,

● rotates his hips to face the rear of the opponent and positions himself for a leg sweep,

● executes the leg sweep by striking the opponent's tendon with the cutting edge of his heel and driving him to the ground,

● returns his right hand to the basic warrior position as he falls,

● keeps his body erect while maintaining control of the opponent's arm,

● executes the heel stomp swiftly and violently to the opponent's head as a finishing technique.

DEFENCES FOR ATTACKS FROM BEHIND

A vital part of a soldier's training in unarmed combat is to practise dealing with attacks from behind. As a rule, a soldier is attacked from behind by an opponent who means to capture him.

If the opponent puts a chokehold on the soldier from behind, the soldier can drop to one knee and use the momentum of his body weight to throw the opponent forward and over. The effect of landing so heavily and unexpectedly should make him an easy captive.

If it proves impossible to throw the attacker over his shoulder – which, given a chokehold could lead to even worse effects on the soldier's neck – the soldier can try blows with his elbow or the edge of his hand. He moves sideways after he has broken free of the hold.

To escape from a bear hug from behind, with his hands and arms immobile, the best thing for the soldier to do is kick the attacker with an upward or backward action in the shins. If the attacker moves his leg back so that the soldier cannot kick his shins, the soldier aims for the knee or the groin instead. A flat-footed kick, especially if the boot soles and heels have hobnails and horseshoe taps, is awfully effective and painful and can even break his leg.

DEFENCE FOR A REAR CHOKE

If the opponent attempts a choke from the rear, the soldier may swiftly and forcefully execute an open-hand groin strike to loosen the choke. To execute this defence, he:

- uses the palm or his hand to strike his opponent's groin and grips the opponent's right wrist with his right hand,
- grabs, squeezes and twists the opponent's testicles forcefully,
- sidesteps quickly to the right under his right arm as the chokehold loosens,
- maintains a firm grip on the opponent's right wrist and violently pulls the opponent's arm to a fully extended and locked position in front of him,
- delivers a powerful left forearm strike to the opponent's elbow once the elbow is in a fully extended and locked position (this damages the elbow and drives the opponent's body down),
- maintains control of the opponent's arm and applies pressure to his injured elbow,
- executes a rear leg front kick to the opponent's face,
- grabs the opponent behind the neck, rotates his hips and executes a leg sweep taking the opponent to the ground,
- executes a heel stomp swiftly and violently to the opponent's head as a finishing technique.

DEFENCE FOR A REAR HEADLOCK

If an opponent applies a headlock from the rear the soldier can gouge the opponent's eyes to loosen the hold. To defend against this headlock:

- the soldier circles his arm over the opponent's leading shoulder,
- reaches as far as possible to prepare for an eye gouge,
- forces his middle finger into the opponent's furthest eye socket (this forces the opponent's head back to expose the throat),
- executes an open-hand groin strike to bring the opponent's hands down, to the groin area exposing his throat,
- delivers a knifehand strike to the opponent's throat as a finishing technique.

LEFT: A kicking attack is stopped when the attacker's leg is caught and lifted high and the defender simultaneously applies a leg sweep forcing his opponent to the ground.

CHAPTER 10

Throws

A throw can only be made within grappling range. A soldier can move in and out of kicking and punching range at will, but once he is in grappling range, he will very rarely get out of it before the end of the fight.

Throws are best avoided as the solider is trained to avoid situations that result in grappling range. He only attempts to throw if he finds himself trapped there with no other options open. The element of surprise is pivotal in the execution of a throw and must always be fast and explosive.

Ideally, the soldier aims to throw the opponent clean and clear of himself. In reality, this is not often what he manages to do, as the opponent is likely to maintain a grip on him even though he's been thrown. He may even pull the soldier down with him. At least the soldier is likely to remain on top.

Of course, the opponent is not placidly going to allow the soldier to throw him, and it could be quite a battle. Throws are far more effective if preceded by feigning a strike, say a head butt, bite or kick. As a singular attack, the throw can quite easily be countered, even by a novice. If, however, the soldier bites his opponent, butts or kicks him before he throws him, his likely success rate improves markedly; so the soldier always tries to distract his opponent with a butt, bite, punch, chop or kick first. If he is pulled down with the opponent, the soldier tries to land on him with the point of his knee, or elbow and break free at the first available moment.

Awareness of surroundings is vitally important, because in a fight, using a fence or railing to trip the opponent's head, or or throwing him back onto it, can make things much easier.

LEFT: Egyptian commandos at the Kuwaiti border fight in the burning sun. Throws are best avoided in a combat situation, however, the soldier must train for all eventualities.

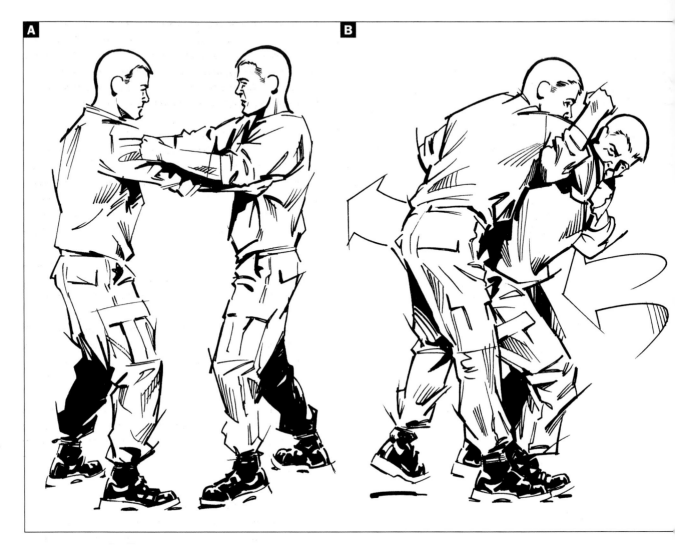

Dropping an enemy to the ground by hitting him in the back from behind or by jumping on him from above, say when he is coming out of a dugout, is an effective and a safer way of overpowering him, throws can be used for defence, attack and escape. In combination with defensive tactics, throws enable a soldier to sustain unarmed combat with an enemy. The most commonly used and effective throws for unexpected attacks are the backward trip-throw, the forward throw over the shoulder and the forward or backward throw by sweeping the attacker's legs out from under him.

Proficient performance of these three basic movements is achieved through continuous, repeated practice in a variety of daily dress, including flak jackets. It is vital to accom-plish throws in a confident manner, even with a rifle slung across the chest or back. This means regular practice of at least five minutes in scheduled and individual training, at least twice a day. Dangerous throws in particular have to be perfected even though they are only practised with dummies.

THE SHOULDER THROW

The forward throw over the shoulder – where one hand lifts the opponent's armpit – is performed with knees bent and with the enemy landing on his head. It may be used on an opponent who grabs from the back as well as from the front. This throw can be executed after a preliminary kick to the groin or with a concluding kick. The soldier breaks

LEFT: The forward throw over the shoulder starts with the soldier gaining a solid grip (A). The soldier breaks the opponent's balance by pulling him towards himself and makes a body turning-in movement as he passes his right arm under his opponent's right arm, gripping hold of his clothes (B). He bends his knees and keeps both feet inside his opponent's then throws him over his right shoulder fast and explosively (C).

KNOCKING HIM OFF HIS FEET

Throws that involve leg grabs are executed together with preceding blows that stun or deter, such as a forearm smash to the nose or head butt at the bridge of the nose. Once he is on the floor he is at the soldier's mercy. An effective way of using a throwing technique to neutralise an opponent is by butting him in the face, then while he is stunned, grabbing his legs from the front and pulling them from under him. The soldier finishes off with a sharp kick to any available target. He can also do this by grabbing the opponent's legs from behind and as he falls forward bring a kick up into his stomach or groin.

Using the inner wrap, a soldier breaks his opponent's balance backward as he wraps his right leg through and around the opponent's lower leg, lifting the leg off the ground. He pushes the opponent – or butts him – violently backward and finishes him off when he is grounded.

In the trip-and-elbow technique, the soldier throws his right elbow into the opponent's face while holding the opponent's right arm with his left arm. The soldier simultaneously wraps his right leg around the opponent's left leg and uses the momentum of his elbow to trip the opponent backward.

From the grappling range, an outside sweep is both simple and highly effective, though it relies, as do all throws, on a fast, explosive attack. The soldier breaks the opponent's balance to his right as he brings forward his left foot. He continues to pull his opponent backwards as he sweeps his right leg to the back of the opponent's right leg to throw him backward. He always tries to precede with a butt, bite or stamp to distract his opponent from the throw.

With an outside ankle throw, the opponent's balance is broken to his right and backward as the soldier places his left foot forward and brings up his right foot. He sweeps the back of his opponent's right heel with his left foot.

In the sweeping ankle throw, the soldier places his right foot forward, forcing the opponent backwards on the left foot. The soldier takes a wide left step as he brings his right foot inward to support his body weight. He breaks the opponent's balance to the right side as he sweeps the

the opponent's balance forward by pulling him towards himself and simultaneously placing his right foot forward towards his opponent's right foot. The soldier makes a body turning-in movement as he passes his right arm under his opponent's right arm, gripping hold of his clothes. He tries to keep both of his feet inside his opponent's and bends at the knees then throws him over his right shoulder fast and explosively.

This kind of throw is used against holds that pin the arms to the body, against holds on the neck and against attacks from behind. The enemy is thrown without any regard for his safety. Whether it is onto some physical object, onto the ground or onto his head, that is not a soldier's concern.

opponent's feet together and lifts him upwards before throwing him with speed and force.

In the body drop, the soldier breaks his opponent's balance to his right and forward. He places his right foot towards his opponent's right foot. The soldier positions his body so that his right foot blocks his right ankle and his left leg is bent. The soldier throws his opponent forward and over the back of his right ankle with speed and as much force as possible.

RIGHT: A combined leg sweep and throw in action. The foremost soldier collapses his opponent's knee from behind by using his calf; at the same time he grips the jacket and prepares to throw the soldier across the sweeping leg and down to the floor.

BELOW: An effective way of using a throwing technique on an opponent is by butting him in the face first (A). Then as he is stunned, grab his legs from the front and pull them from under him (B). The soldier finishes off with a kick in the small of the back (C).

HIP AND THIGH THROWS

The thigh throw is similar to that used in martial arts, but in unarmed combat the right hand grabs not the assailant's clothing, but his throat. With his left hand the soldier holds the opponent by the right arm. He breaks the opponent's balance forward to his right as he places his right foot toward the opponent's right foot. The soldier makes a body turning-in movement so that his left foot is positioned in the centre of gravity then sweeps his right thigh upward on the inside of the opponent's right thigh and continues sweeping his right thigh up and back. The soldier throws the opponent forwards and over his right thigh forcefully.

In the hip throw, the soldier breaks his opponent's balance forward as he brings his right foot towards his opponent's right foot. The soldier turns his body into his opponent's and places his right arm around his opponent's waist or neck. The soldier makes sure that both of his feet are inside his enemy's, his bottom is tightly into the opponent's groin and his knees are bent. He throws the enemy forward fast and explosively over his hip.

In the sweeping hip throw, the soldier breaks his opponent's balance to his right and forward and brings his right foot toward his enemy's right foot. He continues to swing his body into position so that the left foot is positioned in the centre of gravity. He then sweeps the back of his right thigh against the front of the opponent's right thigh, continues sweeping his right thigh backward and throws him forward and over his thigh.

WRIST THROWS

The wrist throw has several practical applications. Its most practical use would be in a situation where a man has reached out and grabbed a soldier's shirt or coat lapel with his right hand. With his left hand, the soldier reaches over and to the inside of the hand between the knuckle bones of his first and middle fingers. The soldier's fingers should pass underneath the palm of his enemy's hand. With his hand in this position, the soldier twists his opponent's hand sharply back toward him and to his right and forces it toward a point on the ground about a metre to his right.

The opponent will immediately be forced to go to the ground and from there the soldier can release his hold on his hand, pulling his arm straight about his head as he goes down. He kicks the opponent in the temple. In cases where the opponent may be much bigger than the soldier, he may wish after making the initial hold with his left hand to use his right to give additional pressure and leverage to complete the throw.

PUSHING COUNTER

Suppose a soldier is in a peacekeeping situation and a belligerent civilian (who may be drunk) attempts to antagonise him by placing a hand on his chest and shoving him backward. The counter is simple and effective. As the opponent's hand is placed on his chest, the soldier takes his own two hands, laying one flat on top of the other, raises them above his opponent's pushing hand and comes down sharply with the edge of the hands at the angular bend where the wrist joins the hand. As the soldier does this, he bends forward and forces the opponent to the ground and also pins the opponent's hand against his own chest in such a manner that the opponent cannot pull away.

The opponent is guaranteed to go down because his wrist is already at a right angle and any additional bend will cause it to break. When the soldier strikes the opponent's wrist with the edge of his hands he can do nothing but go to ground to protect himself from a broken wrist.

As the opponent goes down, the soldier can knee him in the testicles or chin or do whatever he likes.

THROWING A SENTRY

If a soldier is approaching a sentry from the rear, he can apply simultaneous blows across the throat with the forearm and in the small of the back with a clenched fist. With the hand used to strike the sentry in the small of the back, the soldier then covers his mouth and nostrils.

The next move is to slip around to the front, still gripping the sentry around his neck with an arm across his throat, and trip him over one leg, taking him to the ground.

The soldier then lies diagonally across the sentry and transfers his hands swiftly to the stranglehold, one thumb on either side of the windpipe and two fingers of each hand on either side of the spine. Another way is to approach the sentry from the rear and apply a head hold, pulling him down onto your thigh. Keeping him tightly in the hold, the soldier sits down instantly with legs stretched out in front.

RIGHT: For the leg sweep throw, the soldier places his right foot forward, forcing his opponent backwards on his left foot (A). The soldier takes a wide left step and brings his right foot inward to support his body weight (B). He breaks his opponent's balance to the right side, sweeping his feet as he lifts the opponent upwards before throwing him over (C).

CHAPTER 11

Going to Ground

The majority of hand-to-hand fights end up on the ground, which can be a particularly lethal area of combat. Ground fighting is where choking and strangulation techniques are most likely to find application.

The street fighter may be trying to beat his opponent but not necessarily kill him. The soldier, however, is functioning in a different context: it is a kill or be killed situation in which he is seldom trying to take a prisoner. If the goal is to take the opponent out while ground fighting, then these methods have clear advantages and the openings for using them often present themselves.

There are, of course, exceptions to this, but for our purposes the soldier's situation is that his primary weapons have failed – perhaps he has run out of ammunition – or he is attempting to escape and evade. Given these circumstances, the soldier has an advantage over someone using martial arts in a sports competition or a piece of civilian street fighting. He doesn't need to concern himself with intricate, precise manoeuvres. He needs to win. He doesn't need to concern himself with whether he has used excessive force. For him, the right amount of force is that which allows him to survive.

BREAKING A FALL

There may be times during an encounter in which a soldier loses his balance or he is thrown by the opponent to the ground. By using the large muscle groups such as back,

LEFT: Swiss Army soldiers at the Isone Grenadier School practise knee strikes and ground work during a training session.

ABOVE: It is inevitable that a soldier will be thrown to the ground from time to time, and it is imperative that he knows how to fall well. The best way to fall forward is by cupping hands very slightly to absorb the impact. He never falls onto flattened hands.

thighs and buttocks to cushion the impact of a fall and to maintain motion after hitting the ground, he can avoid serious injury and immobilisation.

The soldier tries to use the momentum of a fall to maintain motion. It is important for him to remain in the basic warrior stance, even while falling or being thrown; so he ensures that his head is tucked tightly into his chest. He also reduces his chances of serious injury and increases chances of survival.

He does not throw his arms out to break a fall. This may work well on a mat or in an area with no debris, but in a combat environment he does not know what is on the ground. If he extends his arm and strikes something hard at the elbow, he can effectively take himself out of the fight.

If he needs to fall forward, he cups his hands very slightly to absorb the impact. He never falls onto flattened hands.

THE SHOULDER ROLL

A soldier can use the momentum of a fall to execute a shoulder roll. During a shoulder roll, the large muscle group of the upper back absorbs the impact of the fall rather than the neck and spinal column. To execute the shoulder roll from the basic warrior stance, he:

● tucks his chin and rear shoulder in,
● keeps his arms close to his sides,
● rolls forward,
● continues to roll until he is standing upright,
● resumes the basic warrior stance.

To perfect the technique, he practises the shoulder roll while unarmed and also armed with a rifle.

THE DEFENSIVE PRONE POSITION

Ground work can be split into two categories: grappling on the ground and fighting from the ground. The former is when the soldier and his opponent both fall to the ground. The latter is when the soldier falls, or is knocked to the ground and the opponent is still standing. Both are very dangerous fighting areas for a soldier to find himself in,

RIGHT: Defending from the ground is a precarious skill. A soldier in this position hooks one foot behind the attacker's advancing foot to give himself leverage (A). He then thrusts his other foot into the enemy's shin or groin (A and B). Then the soldier must get up before his opponent can recover, or, kick out rapidly at his groin or knees every time he approaches to attack.

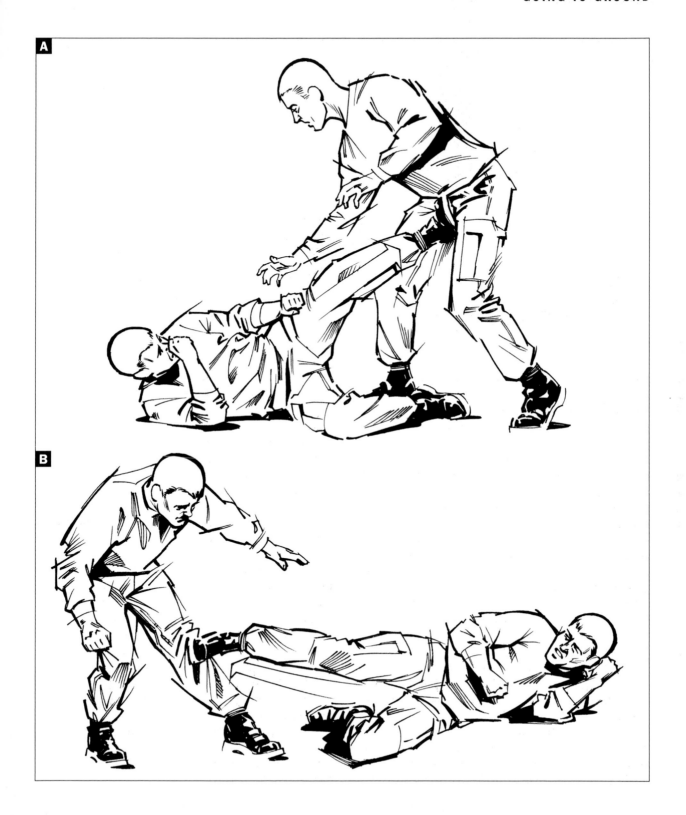

ABOVE: **A Thai Ranger performs a spectacular defence against his knife-armed opponent by gripping the attacker's clothes, rolling onto his back and propelling the attacker into the air with his feet.**

especially the latter. In reality, if the soldier is on the ground and his attacker is standing, his chances of getting back up – especially if he is a novice – are minimal.

Even an experienced fighter faces defeat if he is on the ground. If both combatants fall, or are knocked to the ground, the attacker will almost definitely go in for the kill, so it is imperative for the other that he get himself in a good defensive position. The right knee and right elbow provide cover for the body, groin and head. This defensive prone position defends against attacks while the soldier is on the ground and unable to regain the basic warrior stance. To assume the defensive prone position he:

● positions his body on its side,
● tucks his rear leg under his body for stability,
● places his rear arm under his body with the palm of his hand on the ground,
● moves his rear arm to the right or left while pivoting on his hip to move his body,
● keeps his lead arm in the basic warrior position,
● positions his bicep/tricep area to protect the ribs,
● lifts and cocks his lead leg to protect his groin and strikes the opponent's ankle, shin, knee and groin if necessary.

The soldier makes every attempt to regain his footing and resume the basic warrior stance.

From floor position, the defender hooks one foot behind the attacker's advancing foot to give himself leverage, then thrusts his right foot into and through the attacker's shin or into his groin. Then the defender must get up before the attacker can recover, or kick out rapidly at his groin or knees every time he approaches to attack. As soon as is possible, get up. A soldier should only attack or defend from the ground if he cannot get back up. He should never prefer this ground fighting strategy, it's too dangerous.

ABOVE: If the soldier falls to the ground and his opponent attacks with a kick, he raises his arms and knees in a basic warrior stance to protect his vital organs and uses his arms and hands to absorb heavy blows to the head.

ABOVE: If an opponent manages to get the upper hand in a combat situation and the soldier finds himself on the ground with his opponent on top of him, the most effective way to break free is to wrap his legs around the body – scissors fashion – and wrench the neck.

DEFENCE AGAINST A KICK

If the soldier falls to the ground and his opponent attacks with a kick, the soldier:

- raises his arms and knees in a basic warrior stance to protect his vital organs,
- uses his arms and hands to absorb heavy blows to the head,
- looks for opportunities to make a counter-attack, such as grabbing the opponent's leg and tripping him up.

ASSAILANT ON TOP

If the opponent gets the soldier on the ground and is on top the soldier can break free by getting his legs around the opponent's body, scissors fashion, and wrenching his neck.

If the soldier is pinned down by an attacker working from the side, the left leg can be swung up over the left side of the assailant's neck and used to hook him away from his own grip. The assailant's head can then be held between the soldier's thighs.

Another way of breaking out when the opponent is on top is by applying a chokehold in an overarm head lock with your forearm pressing against his throat. The soldier puts his legs around the opponent's body with a scissors hold and rolls over so that he ends up on his back or

sitting. The soldier squeezes the opponent's body with his legs and bends his head as much as possible.

Or the soldier might start by grabbing the attacker's arms, then roll him over before punching his face. This method relies heavily on arm and body strength but with good technique from plenty of practice it is achievable even if the opponent is much bigger.

SITTING UP

Sitting up, the left leg and knee completely protect the groin and body while the left arm and elbow are ideally positioned to protect the head. The soldier is also well positioned to block oncoming kicks. If the attacker attempts to punch his face, the soldier simultaneously parries the punch and kicks his attacker's left leading leg with his left foot, trapping the leg in place.

The soldier grabs the attacking arm at the wrist with his right hand while at the same time applying an elbow lock with his left hand. He twists the locked arm in a circular motion, throwing his opponent swfitly and violently to the ground. More simply and realistically, he tries to parry off attacks until he can get up from the ground. The longer he stays down the less chance he has of getting back up again.

If the soldier finds it impossible to get back up, he tries to catch hold of the attacker's legs or arms and pull him

LEFT: If the soldier is pinned down by an attacker working from the side, the left leg (in this case) can be swung up over the left side of the assailant's neck and used to hook him away from his own grip. The assailant's head can then be held between the soldier's thighs.

RIGHT: For an assailant on top the soldier should grab the assailant's arms (A) and roll him over onto his back (B). The move is finished off with a punch to his face (C). This method relies heavily on arm and body strength but with good technique it is achievable even if the opponent is much bigger.

down to the ground, where he has a more even chance. If they both fall to the ground it is important that the soldier fights back hard and fiercely by striking him in his vital areas such as eyes, throat and groin, making the attacks calculated and accurate.

FEIGNING SUPPLICATION

If the soldier is severely pinned down and cannot move, feigning supplication is a trick worth trying. By pretending that he has had enough and letting the attacker believe he can have whatever he wants, he can lure the attacker into a false sense of security. If the attacker is foolish enough to leave himself open when releasing the soldier, it is an opportune moment to strike him hard in the eyes or throat with fingers or fist.

CRUCIAL GROUND-FIGHTING STRATEGIES

When he is on the ground, a soldier well trained in unarmed combat:

1 always tries to attack easily accessible vital points and areas which will quickly neutralise the opponent, such as the eyes, nose, throat and groin,
2 tries to use any field-expedient weapons, such as hitting the opponent with a rock, attacking his face or throat with a piece of stick and rubbing dirt, sand and stones in his eyes,
3 (even more crucially) tries to win at all costs, accepting that there are no rules in this life-or-death situation and that anything goes.

LEFT: Another way of breaking out of a situation when an attacker is on top is to get the opponent in an overarm headlock with your forearm pressing against his throat. Put your legs around his body with a scissors hold and roll over so that he ends up on his back or sitting. Follow by squeezing the opponent as much as possible.

Defence Against a Firearm

An unarmed soldier may find himself under threat from an armed assailant and will still need to defend himself. Only he can decide if it is worth risking his life whilst defending himself against an assailant with a gun.

An armed enemy attack can be with a firearm (pistol, automatic weapon, rifle) or cold weapon (knife, bayonet). Under the threat of being shot, a soldier may be searched, secured and taken prisoner. Where it is not possible to use a firearm for defence, the basic actions that can be taken are getting away, bowing to circumstances or fighting back with holds, throws and blows.

Common sense suggests that there is no reliable unarmed defence against handguns – that anything a soldier tries is tantamount to suicide. But sometimes even passive victims who fully cooperate with gun-wielding opponents are wounded or killed, so meek submission isn't always a safe alternative to taking decisive action. There is always the chance of the gun going off accidentally, as in the classic scene in the film *Pulp Fiction* when John Travolta inadvertently blows away the poor passenger in the back of his car.

In addition to the weapon's greater range, the combined shock of noise and flash is a health risk. The blast from a gun, especially in a confined space, can literally deafen and blind a person, not to mention burn someone if it is close

LEFT: Having cautiously approached from behind, a soldier prepares to disarm a guard by pulling his legs out from under him.

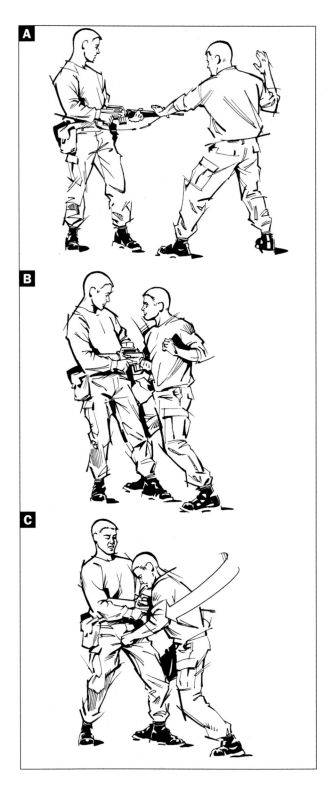

LEFT: Assuming a soldier is within touching distance of a long-barrelled weapon, he can step forward and push it aside (A). He uses one hand to hold the rifle butt underneath his armpit (B) and with his other hand punches the gunman in the face, groin or throat (C).

enough. Because the blast alone makes it likely that a person will be hurt even when successfully defending himself against a gun, a soldier must somehow try to keep the pain from interfering with his ability to execute proper technique.

As a rule, an assault with a firearm consists of a sequence of set actions: threat, approach, waving or aiming the weapon and immediate use either by hitting or shooting. Assessing a situation and choosing tactics and means of defence must generally be done in the stage before an actual attack. There can always be exceptions to the rule, it all depends on the moment. Ultimately, only the soldier can decide if he should risk his life trying to defend himself against a gun.

DEFENCE AGAINST A LONG-BARRELLED WEAPON

Assuming a soldier is within touching distance of a long-barrelled weapon, he can step forward and to the side of his attacker. He grabs the weapon with his leading hand – presumably his left – and pushes it aside. He uses the left hand to push the rifle butt underneath his right armpit and with his left then punches the gunman in the face, groin or throat, depending on which is the most convenient target.

Objects such as headgear, jackets and briefcases can be used for defence. They can be thrown or swung into an enemy's face or against the weapon. Then the soldier can get close to him to use the methods described. For teaching these methods and for psychological conditioning, the instructor's pistol with blanks or a starter's pistol is used.

RIGHT: When a soldier has a gun to the back of his head he slowly lowers himself into a get-ready stance and raises his hands above his head as if willing to cooperate with the attacker (A). Then he quickly pivots on one foot and knocks the gun-wielding arm aside (B). Then he follows up with an elbow strike to the jaw while leaning against the weapon arm (C). He keeps the arm firmly locked to his body, then uses his right leg to sweep the gunman to the ground. The sweep is executed with maximum force by striking the attacker's shoulder with a right heel palm (D). After finishing the sweep, the soldier drops a solid knee strike into his ribs then attacks the throat (E).

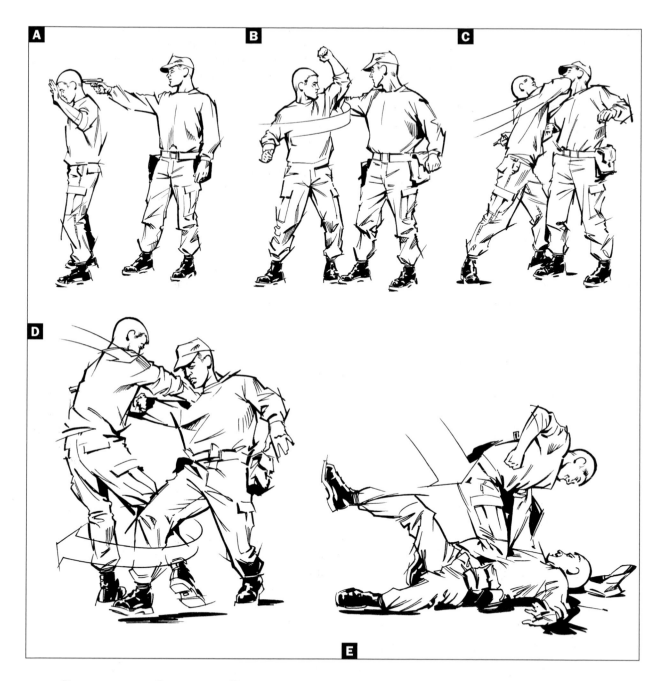

DEFENCE FOR A GUN TO THE FOREHEAD

This dramatic-looking attack is relatively one of the easiest to defend against, because the gun isn't squarely centred on the body. Of course, speed and precision are essential for the soldier to defend against this sort of attack successfully.

The soldier subtly settles into a get-ready stance with knees flexed and tries to bring his hands up in a way that looks like he is cooperating rather than preparing for a counter-attack. As he reaches upward, he readies himself for the necessary defence sequence.

The first move is to duck straight down about half a metre (20 inches). He maintains the same posture as he

DEFENCE AGAINST A FIREARM

ABOVE: An attack from behind is dangerous as the victim is essentially blind. The soldier slowly lowers himself into a get-ready stance and raises his hands in cooperation (A). Then he quickly pivots and loops his left arm over the gun-wielding arm, locking it solidly to his body (B). Following up with a hand strike to the face while leaning against his weapon arm (C).

BELOW: An alternative way of dealing with a firearm attack from behind is for a soldier to raise his arms as if in resignation of capture (A). The soldier should turn swiftly around and knock the gun away from his body (B). The soldier continues to turn around and places his trailing arm over the attacker's gun-wielding arm (C). Then he sweeps the gunman to the ground (D).

bends his knees. At the same time, he brings his right hand straight up, powerfully grabbing the wrist of the attacker's gun-wielding arm.

Then the soldier brings the attacker's hand down in a wrist lock, turning it towards the elbow and then twisting it at an angle. Maintaining a powerful wrist lock, he steps back and pulls the attacker to the ground. He makes sure that the step back is a big one and tries to pull the gunman's arm out of the shoulder socket. In addition to hurting him, this also exposes the ribs in the next phase of the counter-attack.

Prior to locking the attacking hand in place, the soldier steps in and brings all of his weight down on his right knee and onto the gunman's ribs. This will break one or more ribs, causing intense pain and difficulty in breathing. The soldier can then quickly disarm and immobilise him.

DEFENCE FOR A GUN TO THE TEMPLE

As with all gun attacks, this one is extremely dangerous. Yet because of the mobility of the head, the soldier has a good chance of surviving if he executes the following technique quickly and precisely.

Without making eye contact with the attacker, the soldier subtly settles into a balanced get-ready stance with his hands ready for action. He quickly drops straight down at the knees, ducking about half a metre (20 inches). At the same time, he brings his left hand straight up, powerfully grabbing the wrist of the attacker's gun-wielding arm and immobilising him.

Then he brings the attacker's hand down in a wristlock, turning it toward the elbow and then twisting it at an angle.

Maintaining a powerful wristlock, he pivots 180 degrees onto his right foot and pulls the attacker to the ground. He makes the pivot a big one and tries to pull the attacker's arm out of the shoulder socket for the next step in the counter-attack. Then he pins the attacker on the ground with his knee to his ribs and attacks the throat.

DEFENCE FOR A GUN TO THE BACK OF THE HEAD

Any kind of attack from behind, with or without a weapon, is extraordinarily dangerous, because the victim is

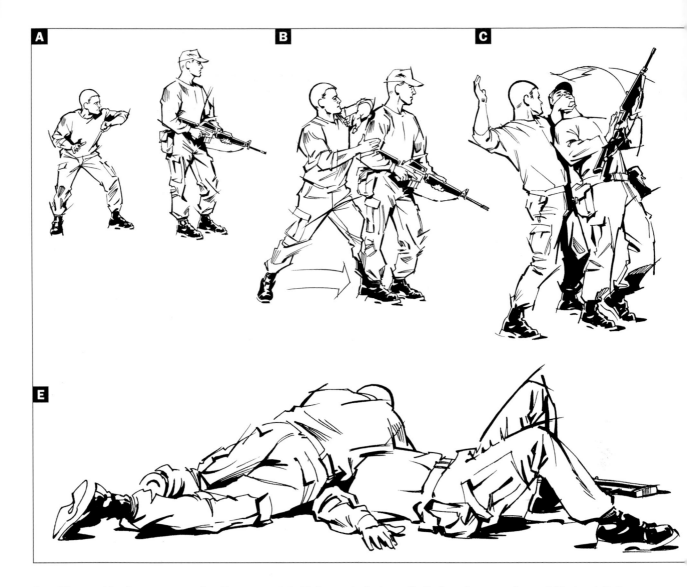

ABOVE: When a soldier disarms an enemy from the rear, great stealth is needed to remain undetected (A). The soldier prepares his leading hand to cover the enemy's mouth (B). The enemy is pulled back with his leading hand and the free hand is used for a smash to the neck (C). The soldier ensures that his left hand stays over the opponent's mouth as the blow lands (D). He follows up as the enemy goes to ground using a choke (E).

essentially blind. The victim can't see the attacker or the way he's positioned. Although 90 per cent of the population is right-handed, the soldier cannot be sure of which hand is holding the gun, so he has to execute a defence technique that's based as much on faith in statistics as anything. This sequence assumes that the gunman is right-handed. As always, the most crucial question is whether he should even try to defend himself in this life-or-death situation. If he does, the following technique should give him a fighting chance of survival.

The soldier slowly lowers himself into a get-ready stance and raises his hands high over his head as if perfectly willing to cooperate with the attacker. Then he quickly pivots on his right foot so that he is facing the gunman. In the same movement, he loops his left arm over the gun-wielding arm, locking it solidly to his body.

DEFENCE FOR A GUN TO THE CHEST

This attack is more dangerous than the gun to the front of the head or the temple because it's harder to avoid the weapon and deflect it safely – the torso is a larger target and less mobile than the head.

After the attacker jams the gun directly into the soldier's chest, the soldier subtly settles into a get-ready stance. The first decisive move the soldier makes is to step forward quickly and to his left and slide his left arm up over the attacker's gun-wielding shoulder. He grabs the attacker's wrist with both hands, locking out his arm.

Then the soldier kicks the left leg out, dropping all his weight on the attacker's arm, taking him to the ground. He follows up with a solid wrist lock that turns the attacker's palm upwards, taking care not to turn the gun toward his own body. This locks out the gunman's shoulder, elbow and wrist, causing him to drop the weapon.

The soldier maintains a powerful wrist lock, controlling the attacker, then picks up the gun and firmly takes control of the situation.

A man who keeps the weapon in his pocket is careless. If the weapon is in his right pocket, he can be suddenly shoved on the point of the shoulder of the gun hand, which in turn will cause his body to pivot so that the gun barrel points away. From here, an alert soldier moves to his rear quickly or to his side, overpowering him and tripping him.

DEFENCE AGAINST A GUN IN THE BACK

If the opponent has placed the flat of his left palm against a soldier's back, with the gun out of range at his hip, the soldier can pivot to the outside, which brings him behind the gunman. There he can secure the opponent's head in his right arm and lock the gun wrist with his left hand, taking the man off-balance.

Now take a walking guard. It is a normal procedure for any guard to want to prod a prisoner in his back while walking. It gives them an air of superiority. To escape, instead of walking in a straight line the soldier plants his left foot to his left at an angle of 90 degrees and pivots quickly. As his forward movement continues, his pivot will bring him to the opponent's rear where he can easily overpower the guard.

In disarming a man from the rear, the soldier must secure the weapon with his left hand while the right arm encircles the opponent's head, bringing him over backward and off-balance.

The soldier instantly follows up with an elbow strike to the gunman's temple while leaning against the weapon arm. He keeps the arm firmly locked to his body, then uses his right leg to sweep the gunman to the ground. The sweep is executed with maximum force by striking the attacker's shoulder with a right heel palm. After finishing the sweep, the soldier drops a solid knee strike into his ribs. Then he attacks the throat.

Besides mastering these techniques, the soldier needs supreme confidence in his ability to make seemingly impossible decisions instantly and accurately. This is all part of the training process for a soldier.

PRACTISING FIREARM DEFENCES

The techniques for unarmed defence against a firearm are the most difficult to perfect simply because they have the most dangerous, if not outright fatal, results if done incorrectly. They must be mastered, however, since the odds are high that a special forces soldier will sooner or later face being held at gunpoint by an enemy.

To make the situation worse, there is no other area in unarmed combat training where so many instructors teach ineffective and inappropriate techniques that, if used by the soldier, will get him killed. There are, in fact, very few methods for safely and effectively handling encounters with a firearm, especially from the front. These few basic methods are taught to elite soldiers around the world, including American special operations and SWAT personnel, the German GSG-9, French GIGN, Israeli Mossad and British Special Air Service counter-terrorists, because they work.

Against firearms the techniques must be fast, effective and, in keeping with the context of soldiering, should end whenever possible with the weapon being used against the attacker to kill or disable him.

Realistically, firearm disarming techniques cannot be learned from a book. Only an experienced instructor can show the nuances of handling such an attack. If a defender makes one mistake in a real-life situation, we all know what the consequences are. There are a few points in general that are worth making in writing about defending against a firearm:

1 When facing a weapon from the front, the only safe way to clear the weapon is to the outside. In other words, if the attacker is holding the weapon in his right hand, the soldier pushes his opponent's weapon hand to the right.
2 Despite what is shown in Hollywood, no one is fast enough to kick a firearm out of someone's hand. The only kick that would work, using the theory of

clearing the weapon to the outside, is an outside crescent kick. This technique is very slow and would be extremely hard to do in a military uniform and boots. Discount all kicking techniques against firearms.
3 Firearm defences are practised against real weapons only when strict safety measures are followed. Both the practice attacker and the practice defender make sure that the weapon is empty. They check both the barrel and the breech.
4 A good test of any technique is for the instructor to

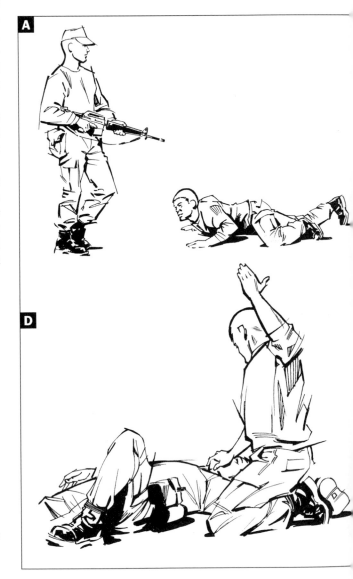

RIGHT: Extreme caution must be used when approaching an armed opponent from the prone position (A). A vicious punch to the groin will have a devastating effect (B). As he doubles up from the pain of the blow, the soldier strikes on the back of the head with a two-fisted blow (C). The enemy will inevitably fall to the ground and the soldier can finish off the move (D). A forearm smash to the neck will totally disable the opponent (E). If there is still resistance the soldier may have to smother his foe (F).

use it against someone in the class. If the instructor, who in theory has been practising the firearm defence for a long time, cannot do it consistently, then perhaps the technique doesn't work. When defending against a firearm, there are no second chances; so finding out whether or not a technique actually works is something to be settled well in advance.

5 When defending against firearms, fancy techniques have no place. Simplicity is the key. Techniques that require a person to switch hands, turn under the attacker's arm, and so on, will not be found on a bat-

tlefield or in a special forces mission behind enemy lines.

6 In a real situation, when the attacker has a firearm and a person decides to defend against it, the attacker will not just stand and watch. This is why soldiers never practise techniques that require an extra second or two where the attacker just stands by as a person defends. The crucial question is always, can the technique be carried out while two antagonists are in motion, or does it require one to be standing still when he pokes the weapon at the other?

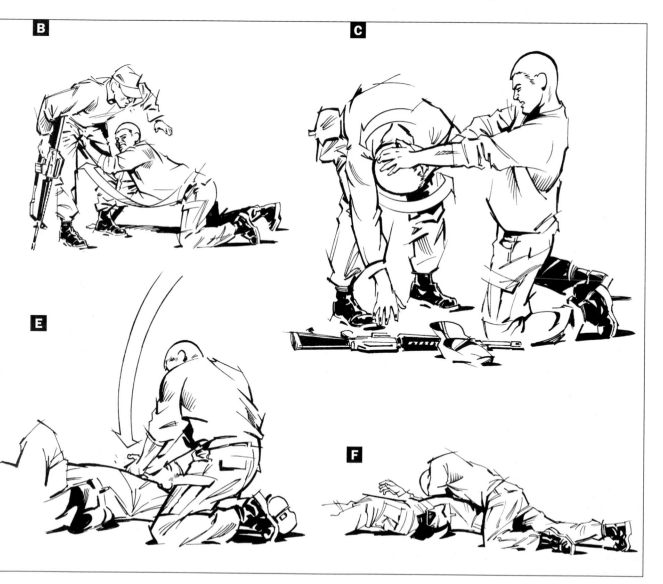

CHAPTER 13

Defence Against Knife Attack

At close quarters, an opponent armed with a knife is perhaps the most lethal enemy a soldier can face. The problem of countering a knife attack is that many conventional blocking techniques would actually be some of the worst counter-measures.

Studies amongst police departments and various military units have revealed that at unarmed combat distance the knife is actually much more dangerous to the defender than someone armed with a gun. The problem of countering a knife attack is that many conventional blocking techniques using the arms would actually be some of the worst counter-measures against a blade. An edged weapon will cut on both thrust and retraction, so if the arm holding a knife is blocked with the defender's forearm the attacker can simply pull the blade backwards and cut deep into the veins of the wrist and arm. Through stabbing or slashing, a knife can quickly inflict lethal blood loss and penetrative injuries and almost any contact between knife and body will open up a wound. The problem is made even more severe for a

LEFT: **Dealing with an attacker with a knife to the throat is a difficult task: the only thing a soldier can be sure of if he is attacked with a knife is that he will be cut.**

soldier in that his opponent may have had formal training in knife-fighting techniques. An experienced knife fighter will not hold his blade in the leading arm, but hold it back out of easy grasp and make rapid attacks in combination with unarmed techniques. He will also use the knife against the defender's vital points, especially the abdomen, thighs and throat where there is major blood supply.

To counter such an appalling threat, the defending soldier must restrict the presentation of his vulnerable points, quickly control the arm carrying the knife and, most importantly, deliver a violent and completely decisive counter technique that will put his opponent down.

Trying to block a knife attack bare-handed may seem futile because the knifeman can move his weapon with lightning speed. If a soldier is attacked by a knife-wielding opponent, the only thing he can be sure of is that he will be cut.

But how badly? Alarming as the idea may be, he knows that it's far better to take a cut on the hand or arm than have his throat slashed or stomach stabbed. Every soldier is aware that in any confrontation against a knife he is likely to be wounded. If by some miracle he isn't, great. But the chances are extremely high that it will happen. Being cut and bleeding, however, doesn't mean that the soldier is out of the fight. If he adopts a defiant attitude then he has an advantage.

Another advantage is the psychology of the person holding the knife. Someone holding a knife in their hand, fully intending to use it as a weapon, tends to rely on the knife at the exclusion of other techniques such as kicks or strikes. Highly trained and experienced soldiers as well as street-smart knife fighters argue that a knife is only one tool that a fighter can use and the odds are not all stacked in his favour. Others say that there is virtually nothing they can do empty-handed against a seasoned knife fighter. They may be right.

The logical solution is for soldiers to be trained to face two types of people. The first is an experienced, deadly knife fighter who most likely will kill an unarmed opponent, barring the miraculous intervention of a fellow soldier, a chance to escape, or a lot of luck. The second is the inexperienced adversary who happens to have a knife in his hand. Many experts in unarmed combat who know a lot about street fighting say that a real knife fighter will never use an overhead stab, or lead with the knife, or wave the knife back and forth in front of a person before he attacks. They are probably right, but a soldier will not be

facing a street fighter. He will most likely face another soldier who happens to be wearing a knife on his belt but has little or no training in its use.

If the soldier hesitates in counter-attacking, he will be giving the knifeman time to set him up for a deadly strike; so quick, decisive action is essential. Against knives the techniques must be fast, effective and, in keeping with the context of soldiering, should end whenever possible with the weapon being used against the attacker to kill or disable him. The soldier must move in on the knifeman as quickly as possible and go for the throat. If the soldier stops his counter-attack before the knifeman is incapacitated, he may get a knife in his back.

Most martial arts techniques, such as high blocks and head-high kicks, can be almost suicidal if applied against a knife-armed opponent. Unless a block is immediately turned into a wrist lock and all kicks directed low beneath the opponent's easy slashing range, then they will simply provide more targets for the aggressor's blade.

DEFENCE FOR A LUNGE
The lunge is a straight-ahead attack that can skewer a soldier's guts if he is not alert and agile. However, as armed attacks go, it's also one of the easier ones to defend against, because the knifeman must be as fully committed as an Exocet missile to make it work well. A soldier executing the following technique with precision will probably be able to turn the tables on the knifeman and render him incapable of causing any further harm.

Suppose the knifeman catches the soldier off-guard, with all of his vital torso targets clearly open to a knife attack. With the knifeman poised to lunge forward, his weapon fully extended, all the soldier can do is keep his eyes fixed on the weapon, flex his knees in preparation and slowly raise his hands for the first move in his counter-attack.

As the knifeman lunges forward, the soldier avoids and deflects the knife by quickly moving aside. He traps the knifeman's forearm against his torso by overlapping it with his left arm. It is crucial that he keeps the knifeman's entire arm trapped very firmly against his body under his left arm because any space can give him enough room to wriggle out of and resume his attack.

LEFT: A US Infantry Division soldier in bayonet training. Notice that the soldier is standing in preparation to attack. Facing a soldier with this advantage would be a daunting prospect for anyone.

RIGHT: If the soldier is close enough to his attacker he may disable him with a kick to the knee or shin (A). The soldier swiftly smashes his leading knee into the attacker's ribs, under his knife-wielding arm (B) (see page 166 for next steps).

the soldier has firmly trapped the arm, he moves his right foot back slightly and twists his stance to the right. This hyperextends the knifeman's elbow joint and may even break it. As he does this, the soldier also begins to apply a solid wristlock in preparation for the next move.

With his arm still firmly holding the knifeman's arm, he places both thumbs in the centre of the back of the knifeman's hand, keeping his left thumb below the right. Then he bends the knifeman's wrist back toward the elbow. He then twists the wrist toward his body. This causes intense pain, perhaps even breaking the wrist. Then the soldier has enough control to execute the next move.

He takes the knifeman to the ground by stepping back and around with his left foot and straightens out his arm while continuing to apply the wrist lock. The soldier makes sure the step is a big one and tries to pull the knifeman's arm out of the shoulder socket. In addition to hurting him, this will also expose his ribs for the next step in the counter-attack.

As he steps in, the soldier brings all his weight down on his right knee and drives it into the knifeman's ribs. This causes intense pain and difficulty in breathing and will also pin him to the ground.

With the right knee firmly planted in the knifeman's ribs, the soldier keeps a tight grip on the knife-wielding hand as he locks it between the chest and left knee. The soldier maintains this lock throughout the final step of the defence sequence.

It may be necessary to attack the knifeman's eyes if he is trying to protect his throat by pushing his chin down against the top of his sternum. The soldier gouges one or both eyes. This will reflexively open up the throat.

Once the throat is open to attack, the soldier uses a spear hand to penetrate around and behind the throat. When he feels the entire structure of the knifeman's throat in his grip, he digs in with his thumb and fingers, squeezing as hard as he can. When the knifeman loses consciousness and is no

The soldier does not try a wrist lock under these circumstances because it is extremely difficult to grab a moving hand precisely. At this point in the defence sequence, all he needs to do with precision is avoid the knife and trap the knife-wielding arm against his body.

The next phase is to hyperextend the knifeman's elbow. This move flows quite naturally out of the last one. After

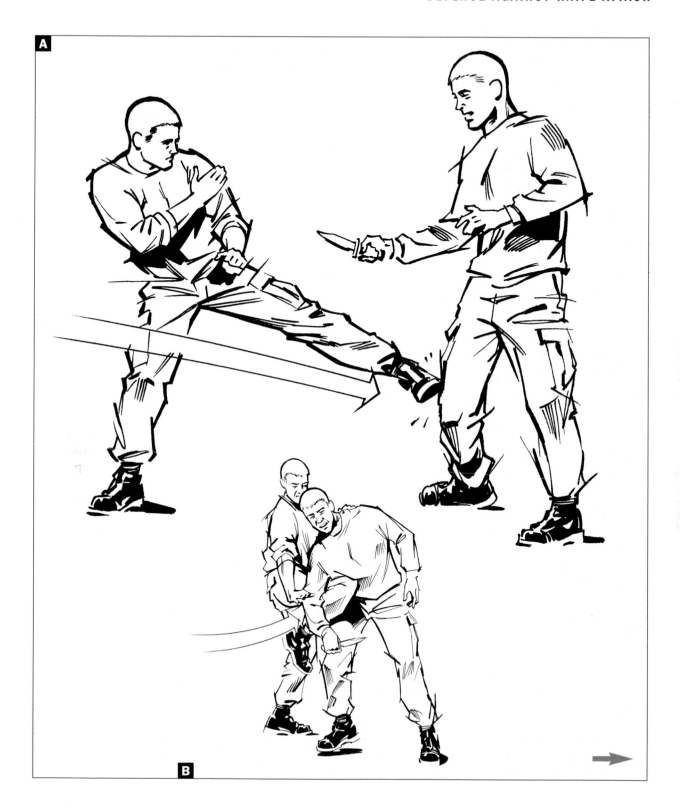

LEFT: Following on from page 165. At the same time the soldier grabs the assailant's arm and twists it with the intention of yanking the knife away from him (C) the soldier uses his body weight and twists his entire body pulling the attacker down to the ground and grab the knife (D). He can follow this move up in any number of way, smothering his assailant or following up with the knife himself.

longer a threat to the soldier's safety, the soldier releases the grip and either escapes or takes the knifeman captive.

DEFENCE FOR A BACKHAND SLASH

Fast circular backhand slashes with a knife seem to come from nowhere, so they can really catch a soldier by surprise. With this kind of sneak attack, a soldier will need to go directly against the knife rather than away from it. Although avoiding the knife is always desirable, he can't do that safely in this case because of the circular motion of the attack. If he ducks the first slash, there will just be more to follow, so the goal is to stop the attack short before it can generate much speed or power and then quickly counter-attack.

In some ways, this attack is less aggressive than the lunge, but it's also sneakier. The attacker may have his arms crossed, concealing the fact that he's preparing to slash with a knife. The soldier's face, neck or throat is the likely target, because a slash won't do much damage to the torso. At this point, all the soldier can do is to stay alert in a get-ready stance, flex his knees and bring his hands up in preparation for the attack. But as soon as he sees the knife he swiftly counter-attacks.

The soldier's first step is to move to the left with arms raised in a double block, with one arm blocking above the knifeman's wrist and one below his elbow. The soldier keeps both blocking arms perpendicular to the ground and makes sure that he does not go too far forward with either arm – that would pull him forward and compromise the stability of his stance.

After completing the double block, he grabs the knifeman's wrist, twisting it downward with his right hand. Keeping his left block planted firmly against the knifeman's forearm, just below the elbow, he delivers a left-heel palm to the elbow, driving it upward. This will do two things. First, it will make a hammerlock much easier to apply. Second, it will drive the knifeman's head and torso up and forward, bringing him up onto his toes and making it much easier to take him to the ground.

With the knifeman off-balance, the soldier applies a solid hammerlock and begins to drive him forward and downward. Using the hammerlock for leverage, he applies pressure with his left elbow to the knifeman's shoulder. As the soldier does this, he drives the knifeman face first to the ground. When the knifeman hits the ground, the soldier continues pushing forward to flatten him all the way out. With the knifeman's face down, the soldier locks his knee against the knife-wielding arm, pinning it firmly to the knifeman's back.

Because the knifeman will be facing down, it's likely that his throat will be inaccessible. If so, the soldier gouges his eyes until his throat is exposed. Once the throat is open to attack, he uses a spear hand to penetrate around and behind the entire throat.

DEFENCE FOR A FOREHAND SLASH

The forehand slash is more aggressive than the backhand slash. However, it's easier to handle because it's a wide circular move. The soldier will have an extra split second, and this will allow him to step inside the attack, block the weapon-wielding arm and set the momentum of the counter-attack.

Assuming that he is facing the knifeman straight on, the soldier settles into a solid get-ready stance with knees slightly bent and hands slightly raised. As the knifeman begins the slash, the soldier steps into a solid double-block stance and hits the knifeman's forearm with the double block, ideally above his wrist and below his elbow.

The soldier grabs the knife-wielding arm at the wrist and begins to neutralise the knife. Depending on the angle of the attacker's head, he immediately strikes the attacker's temple or jaw with his right elbow as he pulls at the knife-wielding arm, bringing the attacker forward.

The soldier wraps his left arm around the weapon-wielding arm, locking it to his side with a wing lock. He makes sure he does this with enough power so that he can spread the knifeman's legs, setting him up for the sweep that follows.

Keeping the knifeman's right arm tightly locked to his body, the soldier uses his right leg to sweep the knifeman to the ground. To get a maximum leverage, the soldier sweeps with his calf against the knifeman's calf. As he finishes the sweep, he follows the knifeman to the ground and drops his knee into his ribs, keeping the knife-wielding hand pinned tightly to his side. If the knifeman's throat is not open to attack, he gouges the man's eyes to help expose this target. When the throat is open, he puts his hand around it and digs in with thumb and fingers, squeezing as hard as he can until the knifeman loses consciousness.

DEFENCE FOR AN OVERHAND STAB

The defence against an overhand stab has to be a precise movement, because there is little margin for error. A soldier who executes it well will be able to control the knifeman. The soldier faces the knifeman from a solid get-ready stance with knees flexed and hands raised to about chest level. He steps forward with his left foot while executing a fast high block. As the soldier makes the block he gets his right hand ready near his right hip, with the fingers up, in preparation for a right heel palm to the knifeman's chin. He controls the knife-wielding arm by applying a wing lock and pinning it to his side. This will set the knifeman up for a sweep. Then he strikes the knifeman's chin with a right heel-palm.

Keeping the knifeman's right arm tightly locked to his body and the heel palm under his chin, the soldier uses his right leg to sweep him to the ground with maximum force. After completing the sweep, the soldier drops a solid knee strike into the knifeman's ribs, keeping the knife-wielding hand pinned tightly to his side. If the knifeman's throat is not open to attack, he gouges the man's eyes to help expose this target. When the throat is open, he puts his hand around it and digs in with thumb and fingers, squeezing as hard as he can until the knifeman loses consciousness.

DEFENCE FOR AN UPWARD STAB

Like the lunge, the upward stab has a straight-ahead line of attack. However, it's harder to follow than the lunge because the weapon comes upward in a sweeping arc. The solution is to defend against the upward stab exactly as if it were a lunging attack, making small adjustments as needed. This is likely to be a sneak attack with the knifeman catching the soldier unawares.

Once again, to prepare himself for a counter-attack, the soldier settles into a solid get-ready stance, flexing his knees and raising his hands. As the assailant begins his upward attack, the soldier avoids the knife and deflects it by quickly moving the knife-wielding arm aside. He overlaps it and traps it with his left arm bent. As with the lunge, it's crucial that the soldier keep the knifeman's entire arm trapped very firmly against his body. That way the knifeman won't have any room to wriggle out and resume his attack. Because this technique has a built-in tolerance for mistakes, the soldier doesn't necessarily have to make a perfect grab

on the knife-wielding hand at this point in the counter-attack. All he needs to do precisely is avoid the weapon and trap the attacking arm against his body.

Then he must hyperextend the knifeman's elbow. As he firmly traps the arm, he moves his right foot back slightly and twists his stance to the right. This will hyperextend the knifeman's elbow joint and either pop it out of place or break it. As he does this move, the soldier also begins to apply a solid wrist lock in preparation for the next move in the sequence, when he positions both thumbs in the centre of the back of the knifeman's hand, keeping his left thumb below his right. He then pivots on his right foot and bends the wrist back toward the elbow twisting it at an angle.

To take the attacker to the ground, the soldier steps back and around with his left foot and straightens his arm out while continuing to apply the wrist lock. He makes sure the step is a big one and tries to pull the knifeman's arm out of the shoulder socket. Then the soldier follows the standard procedure of bringing all his weight down on his right knee into the attacker's chest and squeezing his throat. All the while he continues to hold the knife-wielding hand with his left hand, locking it between his chest and left knee.

DEFENCE FOR A KNIFE-TO-THROAT ATTACK

A knife-to-throat attack is especially dangerous because the weapon is pressing directly against a vital area. Make a mistake here and the soldier is as good as dead. The key to defending against this kind of attack is for the soldier to prevent the knifeman from cutting his throat so he will at least have a chance to counter-attack.

The assailant puts the blade to the soldier's throat as he grabs his opposite lapel. The knuckles of his knife-wielding hand are pressed against the top of the soldier's sternum. From the get-ready stance with his knees flexed for action, the soldier uses both hands to pin the back of the attacker's weapon-wielding hand, pressing it flat against the top of his sternum. This will pull the blade away from his throat and immobilise the hand.

Keeping the hand pinned firmly in place and his feet firmly planted, the soldier twists his shoulders and torso in the direction of the knifeman's thumb. This motion

RIGHT: Thai Rangers practice escaping from a knife attack. This is a seemingly impossible situation to escape from, but by maintaining his cool a soldier can survive this situation.

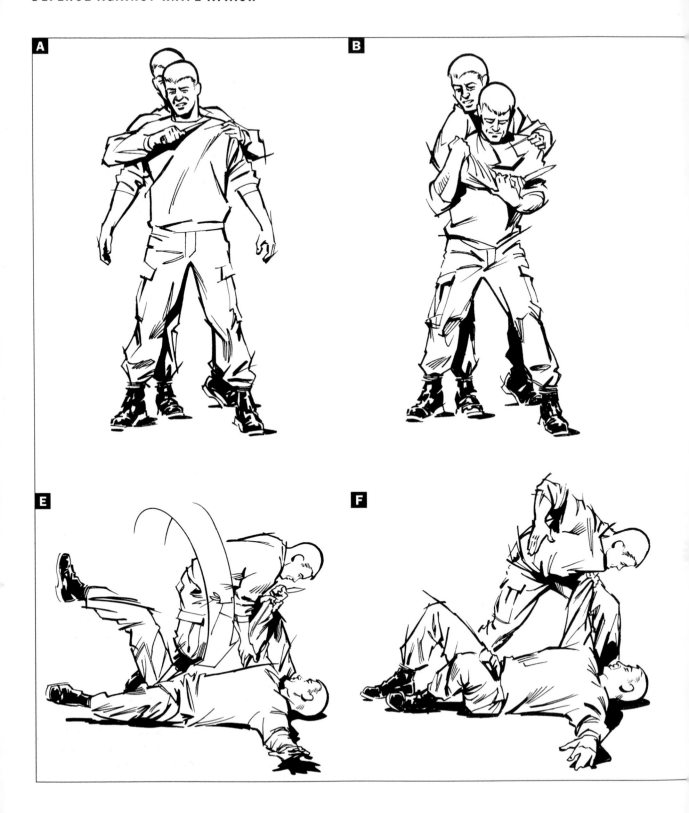

C

D

G

RIGHT: A knife to the throat from behind is arguably the most intimidating attack of all. The attacker comes from behind, grabs the soldier with his free hand and puts the knife against his throat (A). Using both hands, the soldier flattens the knife-wielding hand against the top of his chest so he can't cut the throat (B). At the same time he bends his knees deeply, as if he were preparing to squat (C). He moves his right hand to the attacker's forearm, maintaining a powerful grip on his knife-wielding hand. As he firmly holds the attacker's hand and arm in place, he squats down and bends at the waist, elevating the assailant onto his back (D). Once the attacker is on his way over, the soldier raises his backside as he pulls him directly over his head. He is careful that the weapon-wielding hand and arm don't escape his grip as he flips the attacker. Keeping a tight hold on him will also set him up for the finishing moves (E). After the attacker hits the ground, the soldier firmly locks the knife-wielding hand to his body (F). He smashes the attacker's ribs with his right knee, pinning him to the ground. At the same time, he locks the right wrist between his left knee and chest. Then he finishes him off by attacking the throat (G).

WEAPONS OF OPPORTUNITY

Many weapons of opportunity are part of an everyday environment. A towel or a sock, for instance, when filled with sand, soil, rocks, coins or other heavy objects can act as a very effective cosh which delivers exceptional power because of the sling-like acceleration it achieves when brought against a target in a long swinging arc. In terms of penetrative weapons, keys and pens can level the odds even when fighting against a knife-armed opponent. With the key fob placed in the palm of the hand, each individual key can be sited securely between fingers to form a vicious knuckle duster. A pen/pencil has a similar value. Attacking the opponent's neck and temples with a pen is a potentially lethal technique. If the pen/pencil is especially sharp, or you have a sharpened stick, a non-lethal alternative is to drive it deep into the opponent's thigh – the subsequent pain is extraordinary and will almost certainly incapacitate the attacker. Other readily available items to use in combat are cigarette lighters and hair combs – the former can be used to break an enemy's lock hold while the latter delivers a painful slash when drawn across the face or arms.

Bottles are a long-standing weapon of street fighting, and they can have an equal value to a soldier. However, bottles are more effective weapons when used as a club rather than attempting to smash the end off the bottle and use it as a slashing weapon. Trying to break the end of a bottle will usually result in the bottle shattering and the holder receiving potentially dangerous lacerations to the hand. A much more effective club available to many soldiers is a heavy military torch. SAS soldiers are trained in using their solid rubberised torches as attacking weapons, and a torch also has the advantage that its beam can be used to temporarily blind an assailant.

Rocks and soil are often readily available in outdoor fight situations and can be used to knock an opponent out or blind him by throwing dirt into his eyes. Whatever the weapon of opportunity, the soldier must have the awareness not to make it the sole method of attack. The enemy's concentration will immediately fasten on the weapon and thus he will leave himself open to conventional unarmed techniques which do not involve the offensive tool. Improvised weapons are best used as part of the soldier's general unarmed attack and not as a limitation of his skills.

should break his wrist. While he is executing this move, he makes sure that he keeps his shoulders level and doesn't bend over.

Going with the momentum of the twisting motion initiated in the previous move, the soldier grabs the knifeman's hand with both of his. He places his thumbs directly in the centre of his attacker's hand, keeping his left thumb below his right. He bends the knifeman's wrist back toward his elbow, then twists it an angle.

The soldier maintains the wristlock and continues moving in an arc. As he steps back with his left foot, he stretches the knifeman's arm out to expose the ribs as he grounds him. He breaks the knifeman's ribs with his knee as he pins him to the ground. At the same time, the soldier pins the knifeman's right wrist between his left knee and chest. He should then have the knifeman's throat at his mercy.

DEFENCE FOR A KNIFE TO THE THROAT FROM BEHIND

Arguably the most intimidating attack of all is a knife to the throat from behind, because the soldier is not facing the attacker and he will be counter-attacking from a blind position. Again, the key to defending is for the soldier to prevent the knifeman from cutting his throat before he has a chance to swing into action.

The knifeman comes from behind, grabs the soldier with his free hand and puts the knife against his throat. Using both of his hands, the soldier flattens the knife-wielding hand against the top of his chest so that the knifeman can't cut his throat. The soldier makes sure that he does the pin with his left hand first, then his right. At the same time as he executes the pin, he bends his knees deeply, as if he were preparing to squat.

He moves his right hand to the knifeman's forearm, maintaining a powerful grip on the knife-wielding hand. Firmly holding the knifeman's hand and arm in place, he squats down and bends at the waist, elevating the knifeman onto his back. He is now ready to catapult him onto the ground, head over heels.

Once the knifeman is on his way over, the soldier raises his backside as he pulls the knifeman directly over his head. He is careful that the weapon-wielding hand and arm don't escape his grip as he flips the knifeman. Keeping a tight hold on him will also set him up for the finishing moves. After the knifeman hits the ground, the soldier wraps his arm around his, firmly locking the knife-wielding hand to his body as he bends down toward him. Going with the flow, he breaks the knifeman's ribs with his right knee, pinning him to the ground. At the same time, he locks the knifeman's right wrist between his left knee and chest. Then he finishes him off by attacking the throat.

PRACTISING KNIFE DEFENCES

When practising these defence techniques, soldiers usually wear safety goggles and use rubber knives. Alternatively, one practice method for teaching the soldier how quickly a knife fight can turn serious is a variation of a training drill used in the movie *Spartacus*. In the film, lethal body sword cuts are demonstrated and then practised using a large paintbrush dipped in paint. Instead, this drill uses the largest magic marker available.

One soldier attacks another using the magic marker as a knife and using it in many different ways, such as slashing and stabbing. This first happens early in a soldier's training, when trainees have not mastered techniques for defending themselves against knife attacks. Usually the defender is covered with pen marks where a real knife would have cut him with potentially fatal consequences.

Then after the soldiers have trained for a while in knife-defence techniques, the magic marker drill is used again. The soldiers are able to see how many fewer marks their enhanced skills have allowed them to escape with. They are also able to see to what degree they are not invulnerable – to what degree they must continue to respect an enemy with a knife.

PRINCIPLES OF DEFENCE AGAINST KNIFE ATTACKS

Techniques for defence against knife attacks incorporate the following strategic points:

1 The weapon hand must be controlled as soon as possible.
2 The attacker must be neutralised with a disabling or killing technique.
3 If possible, weapons of opportunity and diversions should be employed, such as kicking sand or throwing something in the attacker's face, or choking, striking, or poking him in vital areas with a long piece of wood or pipe.
4 When possible, the attacker's weapon should always be used as the fastest means to neutralise him. The soldier doesn't need to worry about legalities, only survival.

MILITARY KNIVES

Because of their dual purpose for both combat and utility, military knives and bayonets are some of the best constructed edged weapons in the world. The knife is an extremely important part of the equipment of an elite soldier. In the field it is useful for digging holes, opening tins and cutting wood for fires. The actual blades usually have a base metal of carbon steel or stainless steel (mixed with other steels such as molybdenum, chromium and vanadium), the former giving a sharper edge but the latter resisting rust more efficiently and giving a longer-lasting edge. The choice of metal is important to how a knife performs in combat. Other blades, such as the bayonet for the Russian AK-series of firearms, also come with their own wire-cutting mechanism.

A potential problem is the knife's temper. If a knife is under-tempered it could shatter in use. A full tang (the extension of the blade which fits into the handle) will substantially improve the weapon overall, as it makes the knife considerably stronger. Military knives are primarily intended for non-combat use, though they are also designed to be an extremely competent weapon should the need arise. Regardless of the exact model used, all special forces knives have similar characteristics. They all have a blade guard, which provides protection for the hand, plus a finger spot, which the little finger wraps around when holding the weapon for defence. The handle itself is hard so it can be used for striking. Most military knives have two cutting edges, though the top edge is usually serrated so that it can be used as a saw. Maintaining the blade's sharpness is imperative, and it is normal for troops to carry a small stone for such a purpose. Sharpening a blade involves maintaining an even pressure across the full width of the edge of the blade (elite troops spend a great deal of time sharpening their knives – a blunt knife is not just an inefficient tool, it is also a dangerous liability to its owner).

The knife's grip is extremely important as it determines whether the user will have exact and secure control of the blade. If a grip is too large it is difficult to hold onto; if too short the user may have difficulty in holding the knife correctly – potentially lethal in a close-quarter combat situation. Generally special forces soldiers go for a grip that is slightly too big, because it is less tiring to use and makes the knife easier to hold when wearing gloves.

CHAPTER 14

Defence Against Bayonet Attacks

An opponent armed with a bayonet is a deadly adversary. The first step of unarmed defence against a bayonet is to neutralise the weapon. The most effective way is to damage the opponent's arms.

I t is a popular misconception aided by Hollywood movies that elite troops kill their opponents using a bayonet or knife most of the time. The reality is that these weapons are rarely used and when they are it is as a last resort, the consequences are quite likely to be fatal. However, it is still imperative for a soldier to know how to defend himself if faced, unarmed, against a opponent with a bayonet. The most effective way is to damage the opponent's arms, confronted with a slash or a straight thrust, a soldier neutralises the opponent's lead arm, he can then follow up with a counter manoeuvre. If confronted with a smash or with horizontal or vertical butt strokes, he neutralises the opponent's rear hand. Once the bayonet is neutralised, he attacks the opponent using the standard unarmed combat techniques.

LEFT: A forearm smash to the face quickly stuns an adversary. Defending against a bayonet is not an easy thing and a soldier will need to react quickly to stand a chance. However, success can be achieved with the correct technique and level thinking.

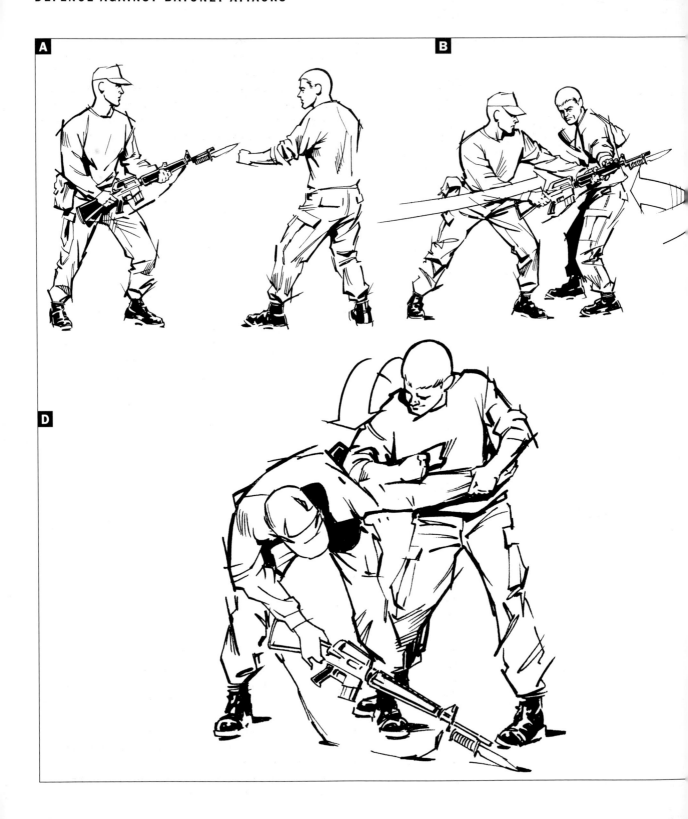

C

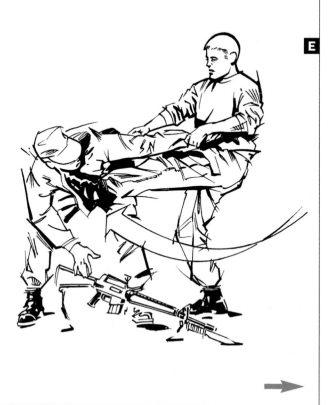

E

Left: **In an unarmed defence against a bayonet attack the first step is to neutralise the bayonet. As the opponent attacks (A) the soldier steps in quickly to execute a lead-hand parry to the opponent's lead arm (B). He pushes the opponent's arm away and down to the left. Then he grabs the opponent's lead wrist with his lead hand (C). The soldier executes a rear forearm strike to the opponent's elbow to neutralise the arm (D). He then applies pressure to the arm with his forearm to force his head down for a kick to the face (E).** **See page 178 for next steps.**

COUNTERING A BAYONET SLASH

The soldier assumes the basic warrior stance and as the opponent attacks with the slash, he:

- steps in quickly to execute a lead-hand parry to the opponent's lead arm,
- pushes the opponent's arm away and down to the left,
- grabs his lead wrist with his lead hand,
- executes a rear forearm strike to the opponent's elbow to damage and neutralise the arm,
- applies pressure to the opponent's arm with his forearm to force his head down for a kick to the face,
- executes a rear-leg front kick to the opponent's face,
- grabs the opponent behind the neck with the lead hand,
- grips the opponent's injured arm with his rear hand,
- rotates his hips and executes a leg sweep to take the opponent to the ground,
- executes the heel stomp as a finishing technique.

COUNTERING A STRAIGHT THRUST

The soldier's way of countering the straight thrust is first to assume the basic warrior stance. Then he:

- steps to the right quickly,
- executes a lead-hand parry to the opponent's lead arm,
- grabs the opponent's lead wrist with his lead hand,
- executes a rear forearm strike to the opponent's elbow to damage and neutralise his arm,
- applies pressure to the opponent's arm with his forearm to force his head down for a kick to the face,
- executes a rear-leg front kick to the opponent's face,
- strikes the opponent behind the neck with his lead hand,
- grips the opponent's injured arm with his rear hand,
- rotates his hips and executes a leg sweep to take the opponent to the ground,
- executes any number of ways as a finishing technique.

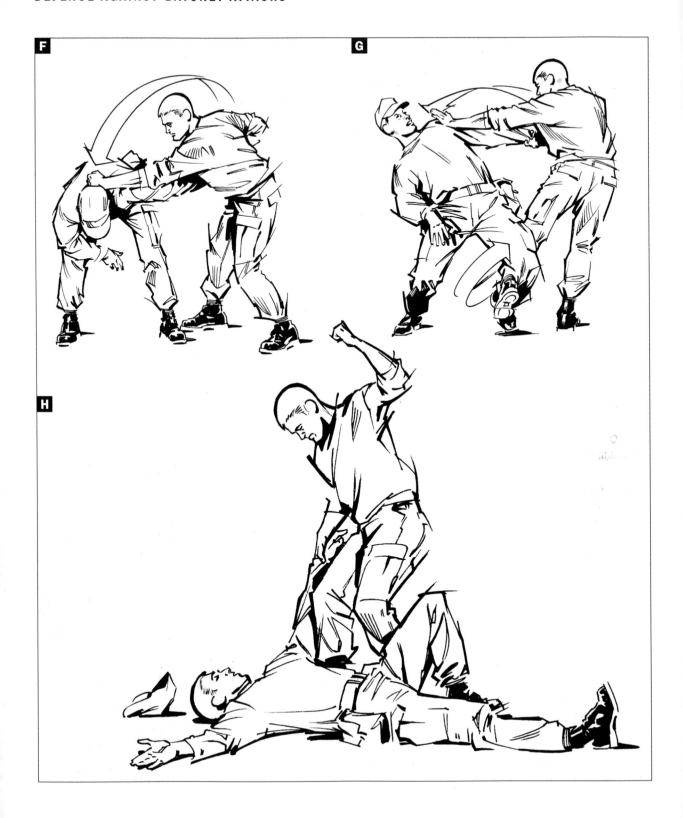

LEFT: **Following on from page 177. Then he grabs the opponent behind the neck with the lead hand (F), and grips the injured arm with his rear hand, rotates his hips and executes a leg sweep to take him quickly to the ground (G). A punch to a vulnerable area or a heel stomp can be used as a finishing technique (H).**

Suppose infiltrating enemy troops suddenly rise from the edge of a cleared command post area and charge, intending to bayonet someone standing there. If the target has been trained for this situation and has presence of mind to use his training, he will drop into a crouch, raise the arms with fists clenched, fingers toward the face and wait for the inevitable thrust.

Depending on what section of the upper body area the thrust is aimed for, the man under attack will strike the flat side of the bayonet a sharp blow with the inside of the forearm, pivoting his body out of thrusting range. The forward movement of the attacker will carry him past the target, who will then seize the upper handguard of the attacker's rifle with both hands. Since the target has already pivoted his body to the left, he can now strike his attacker a sharp blow with the sole of the foot against the knee or groin and wrench the rifle out of his grasp or trip him in front of his feet, destroying his balance.

COUNTERING A HORIZONTAL BUTT STROKE

The soldier assumes the warrior stance, then:

- steps to his left quickly,
- executes a rear-hand parry to the opponent's rear arm,
- pushes the opponent's arm away and down to the right,
- grabs the opponent's rear wrist with his rear hand,
- executes a lead forearm strike to the opponent's elbow to damage and neutralise the arm,
- applies pressure to the opponent's arm with his lead forearm to force his head down for a kick to the face,
- executes a rear-leg front kick to the opponent's face,
- grabs the opponent behind the neck with his rear hand,
- grips the opponent's injured arm with his lead hand,
- rotates his hips and executes a leg sweep to take the opponent to the ground,
- executes a heel stomp swiftly and violently as a finishing technique.

RIGHT: **Soldiers practising a butt stroke. A special forces soldier needs to know how to use his equipment in any number of ways.**

COUNTERING A VERTICAL BUTT STROKE

The soldier assumes the basic warrior stance, then:

- steps to his right quickly,
- executes a lead-hand parry to the opponent's rear arm,
- pushes the opponent's arm away and to his right,
- delivers a palm strike to the inside of the rear elbow with his rear hand (this creates a gap between the opponent's torso and rear arm),
- moves his lead hand under the opponent's rear arm to the back of his neck,
- releases the opponent's arm and rapidly moves his rear hand over the rear shoulder to the back of the neck (this controls the opponent's rear arm),
- applies pressure to the opponent's locked rear arm and neck to force his head down,
- executes a knee strike to his face,
- grabs the opponent behind the neck with his rear hand,
- grips the opponent's wrist with his lead hand,
- rotates his hips and executes a leg sweep to take the opponent to the ground,
- executes a heel stomp as a finishing technique.

CHAPTER 15

Defence Against Clubs and Truncheons

Although it seems unlikely, clubs and truncheons can be equally as dangerous as knives. They can easily crush arm and leg bones, not to mention skulls. They can give the attacker greater striking range because of their length – even a short club is longer than a bowie knife.

Ironically, though, the closer a soldier can get to a club, the better. The longer range of the club makes it less effective as an in-fighting weapon than a knife. Although techniques taught in a bare six weeks of training will cover only the most common truncheon and club attacks, they normally provide the basic moves needed to defend successfully against variations that might come a soldier's way. The most important point is that, to survive such an attack, the soldier focuses on taking away the reach advantage that the weapon gives the attacker. To defend against the truncheon-wielding attacker, the soldier must close the distance instantly and counter-attack with complete accuracy and maximum power. A moment's hesitation, one wrong move and the attacker can pulverise his opponent.

LEFT: The use of the baton and night stick is just as important in the application of non-deadly force or restraint. A soldier must be trained in the use of all methods of unarmed combat.

LEFT: Soldiers practise defending against attacks with clubs. Defending against a club or a truncheon can be as dangerous as defending against a knife. A club can crush a skull or break a leg and an attack of this nature can be very aggressive.

block as a weapon that can break the weapon-wielding arm. At the same time, he get his right hand ready near his right hip, with the fingers pointed up, in preparation for a right heel palm to the chin.

He firmly controls the assailant's weapon-wielding arm by wrapping his left arm around it, locking it to his side. As he does this, he moves the assailant to the left, spreading his legs and setting him up for a sweep. He simultaneously strikes the assailant's chin with a right-heel palm. Keeping the assailant's weapon-wielding arm tightly locked to his body, he uses his right leg to sweep him to the ground. This sweep is done with maximum force by striking the assailant's shoulder with a heel palm to accelerate his fall.

DEFENCE FOR A FOREHAND CLUB ATTACK

A forehand club attack is very aggressive. It is similar to the forehand slash with a knife, except the reach and power of the club makes it even more dangerous. The key to defending against this kind of attack is for the soldier to get inside the club's circle of death quickly and block the weapon-wielding arm. Although the soldier's natural instinct may be to back up when attacked with a raised truncheon or club, that can be more dangerous. No determined attacker will stop after one swing. He'll chase his target down, swinging repeatedly, until he connects. Rather than waste time and energy stumbling backward, the soldier needs to move instantly toward the attacker.

The soldier positions himself for a counter-attack by getting into a solid get-ready stance with knees slightly bent. He brings both hands up near the centre of his body. As the assailant begins the slashing motion, the soldier hits the assailant's forearm with a powerful double block, above the wrist and below the elbow. Then he grabs the weapon-wielding arm at the wrist to begin to neutralise the truncheon or club. Then, depending on the angle of the assailant's head, he immediately strikes the assailant's temple or jaw with his right elbow as he pulls his right arm forward.

To firmly control the weapon-wielding arm, he wraps a left wing lock around it, locking it to his side, making sure

DEFENCE FOR AN OVERHAND CLUB ATTACK

An overhand club attack is very similar to an overhand knife attack, so the defence is virtually the same. The main difference is that the soldier must be sure not to whiplash the weapon onto his head when making the block.

The assailant will probably initiate this attack with an extremely powerful strike to the head, although he may also aim for the collarbone. To prepare to defend, the soldier faces the assailant from the usual get-ready stance with hands raised to about chest level. Then he steps into a blocking stance while executing a powerful outward high block. It's important for the soldier to think of the

he does this with enough power so he can move the assailant to his left. This will spread the assailant legs and set him up for the sweep that follows.

DEFENCE FOR A BACKHAND CLUB ATTACK

A backhand club attack is similar to the hidden-hand attack with a knife. The soldier will be taught that the faster he closes the gap between himself and the assailant and the closer he can get to the club without being hit, the safer he is. He will be taught to keep in mind that although this backhanded strike will most likely be aimed at the head, it might also be aimed at arms and ribs, in which case he will

ABOVE: To repel an overhand club or truncheon attack the soldier should execute a powerful high block immediately followed by a right-heel palm to the chin. He should then wrap his arm around the assailant's weapon-wielding arm and sweeps him to the ground.

have to adjust his block.

The technique practised is the same as for the knife attack – executing a double block, grabbing the attacker's wrist, twisting it and delivering a heel palm to the elbow. The soldier applies a hammerlock, executes a takedown, then locks the weapon-wielding arm before attacking the eyes and throat.

CHAPTER 16

Multiple Assailants

Fighting is not always about being fast, strong, accurate or even brave, though they are all, of course, important factors. It's often about being the first to make a move. This is especially true in dealing with two, three or more attackers.

When a well-trained soldier faces more than one attacker he should initiate the fighting if he can, so that he is in control. If he waits for his assailants to make the first move, he will most likely be hospitalised or killed. When they do attack, it will not be one at a time, each in succession. It will be all of them at once and they will be brutally ferocious, leaving the soldier very little chance of fighting back.

A special forces soldier is taught to think and act fast in this situation, because as the seconds tick by the attackers will be getting closer, and for every second that he delays his first pre-emptive strike, he will be fighting one more opponent. To manage the pivotal seconds effectively, his first attack will be to the opponent in front, then to the next opponent. If he mismanages that vital time his strategy must change. The absolute imperative in such a scenario is to attack first, attack being the best means of defence. After his pre-emptive strike, it is best for the soldier to make his getaway, if possible – otherwise he hits everything that moves and screams to underline his resolve, to psyche out his antagonists. Which target he chooses to attack depends on the circumstances.

LEFT: Experts from the Soviet Spetsnaz put on a demonstration of unarmed combat techniques, using hands and feet to repel and defeat an opponent, to a motorised infantry unit in Afghanistan during a break from operations.

ABOVE: **Facing multiple attackers is as dangerous as it gets in the world of unarmed military combat. In the three–one situation the single defender must initiate the attack. He needs to manoeuvre the situation so that one of the attacker's is distracted (A). The soldier may need to execute a fast eye jab (B) to get his attention while the real focus of attack is one of the outer opponents (C). He then sets about taking out the other attackers (D) See pages 187 and 188 for next steps.**

Whatever it is, it will be the best shot he can aim at a vulnerable area such as the eyes, throat, groin or jaw.

IMPROVISATION IS THE KEY

To have any hope of surviving a fight with a group of armed, highly trained soldiers, a soldier needs to have practised techniques that can somehow bring order out of chaos and allow him to escape with his life. Facing multiple attackers is as dangerous as it gets in the world of unarmed military combat. Against multiple attackers, the soldier may be forced to improvise, using old techniques in new and different ways. Also, unlike the defence against one attacker, with multiple attackers he absolutely must stay on his feet. If he makes the mistake of going to ground to finish one attacker, the others will descend on him with murderous rage. If he is knocked to the ground, he gets back up immediately.

The key to the soldier's survival is that he is single-minded in his selection of targets and weapons, concentrating on counter-attacks to the eyes and throat. Even though the danger level increases with each additional attacker, the situation is not necessarily hopeless if the soldier starts with a sound defence strategy and uses only the most effective techniques quickly, precisely and relentlessly.

STRATEGIES AND TACTICS

Although multiple armed attackers equal big trouble, a well-trained soldier does not succumb to negative thinking. Rather than being fatalistic about facing this kind of encounter, he gives himself a fighting chance by sticking to a practical strategy based on simple, powerful counter-attacks against each weapon-wielding attacker.

He already knows that going to the ground with one attacker when there are others who can stab, beat, or shoot him is tantamount to suicide, but when facing multiple attackers there's an equally important concept to keep in mind, which is that he cannot engage any individual attacker for any longer than it takes to incapacitate him.

If he is going to use one attacker as a shield against the others, he simultaneously attacks his eyes or throat. As soon as he's no longer a threat, the soldier disposes of him and

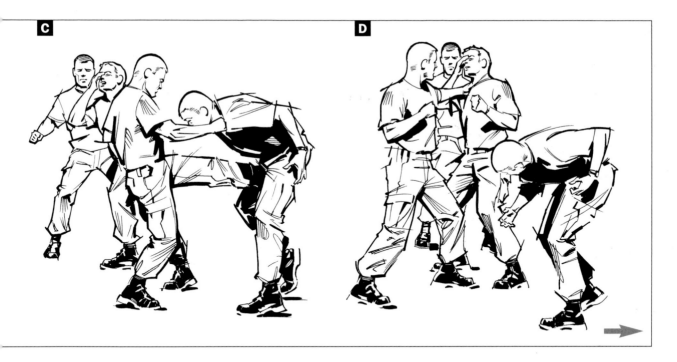

pursues the next attacker, repeating the same sequence of shielding himself with the assailant as he finishes him off.

Although it may not be the case, the only safe assumption he can make is that if one attacker is armed, then all are armed. That means he defends himself against each individual with the same ruthlessness he would normally reserve for weapon-wielding assailants. He takes this attitude because an attack by multiple assailants can be deadly even if none of them is armed. In the vast majority of cases, superior numbers alone give a group the advantage it needs to maim or kill a single defender. And the moment even one weapon makes an appearance, the ferocity of the attack escalates drastically, so the soldier pulls out all the stops in order to have any chance. The extra confidence members of the attacking group will have can be destroyed if even one is incapacitated.

DEFENDING AGAINST TWO ATTACKERS

This is more than double trouble, because two attackers can come at a soldier in a number of different ways – side by side, from in front and behind and from varying angles. The best strategy for the soldier is to align them so that they are shoulder to shoulder. If the soldier can't see both of them clearly at all times, he won't be able to hit key targets and it will be much easier for them to overwhelm him.

It may seem strange to speak of aligning the attackers the way you want them, but if a soldier is trained to keep that goal in mind, he has a chance to accomplish it. The best way to get two attackers shoulder to shoulder is to visualise them as points on a line and manoeuvre them accordingly. This takes some deft footwork.

By keeping both attackers directly in front of him, the soldier protects his back and flanks, making the threat more manageable. Once he's got them where he wants them, he counter-attacks quickly and decisively. He moves toward the nearest assailant, neutralising his weapon and crushing his throat. At the same time, he can use this assailant as a shield against the other. Once he's quelled the threat of the first attacker, he disposes of him and does the same to the second.

This is not an easy or certain process, but with a workable plan in mind, a trained soldier at least has a viable alternative to panic and capitulation. By disrupting the attackers' plans and vigorously counter-attacking, he has a legitimate fighting chance of survival.

One other important thing for a soldier defending against a group attack is to pick up on the social dynamics of the force arraigned against him or her. Most groups, even those of professionally trained soldiers, will tend to have a leader which the others follow, if only in a strategic

ABOVE: **Following on from pages 186 and 187. Now the outer assailant is occupied, the special forces soldier uses the middle assailant as an obstacle between himself and the remaining attacker (E) by shoving him forcefully into the attacker (F). The soldier then needs to finish off the attackers as quickly as he can with a swift punch and a kick.**

sequence of attack. The leader may well give himself away by initiating all attacks, being the most verbal of the aggressors or simply showing the most confidence (though soldiers operating in civilian environments should also be aware that a silent or unobtrusive-looking member of a gang could be allowing his noisier colleagues to set up his attack). If the leader is identified and escape from the group is impossible, then the soldier should attempt to take out the leader with as aggressive a technique as possible. If this is done successfully, the violence of the leader's dispatch may well deter the others from launching their assaults and may also deprive the group of their tactical coherence.

Escape and evasion are the other key maxims of defence against a group. The defender should always keep on the move to disallow construction of an encirclement pattern around him by the attackers. By moving erratically and attacking each of the group members hard when they come into contact, a gap may be created through which

the defender can simply run and outpace his opponents. However, the soldier should be aware of two things when running away. One, have the defenders any firearms which they have so far not used because of the close ranges and the danger to their colleagues, which could be used if the defender puts himself at some distance from them? Two, the running soldier should always listen to the pattern of footsteps behind him. If they are getting louder, that means his opponents are gaining on him and he should turn and fight once more.

DEFENDING AGAINST THREE ATTACKERS

As with two assailants, three can attack in any number of ways. The soldier under attack tries to manoeuvre in such a way that all three are on a line and he is on the apex of a triangle opposite that line. Ideally, the defending soldier should make his initial attacks to the assailant's at each end of the line to stop the line wrapping around him. However, this is not always possible and most often the soldier will just have to deal with each opponent as they come. This can be made easier by constant movement, which breaks up the integration of the attacking group and makes each attacker approach singularly rather than as part of a pack. Thus separated, the group is more vulnerable and the defender should then take out each opponent with hard techniques.

DEFENDING AGAINST A LINE OF ATTACKERS

If a soldier is attacked in a confined area like a narrow alley, he may have to deal with a line of attackers. He is actually at a slight advantage here, because without lateral room to attack his flanks, the assailants will tend to pile up on each others' backs.

If that happens, he has a chance of handling them one by one. If he can instantly control weapons and strike vital targets, he may be able to slide by and escape. To pull this off, he has to improvise like a jazz musician – just so long as he sticks to the right scale. He knows the notes that he needs to play, such as striking eyes and crushing throats, but it's up to him to decide how to put them together. Ultimately, the degree of his effectiveness in orchestrating a successful sequence of defence techniques will determine whether his composition is a masterpiece or a dirge.

DEFENDING AGAINST A CIRCLE OF ATTACKERS

The only way to survive a circle of armed attackers is to break down the circle's structure immediately, which gives the soldier a chance of protecting his back and flanks.

To break the circle, he standardises his counter-attack by moving against the assailant standing closest to his left. The soldier immediately neutralises the assailant's weapon while crushing the man's throat and using him as a shield against the rest. The process then becomes the same as with the other multiple-assailant scenarios in this chapter. The soldier can only deal with one attacker at a time, but he does it with ruthless efficiency. Only when he has neutralised the attacker he is focused on can he move on to the next and the next.

LEAVING A MARK

The subject of defence against multiple attackers is a grim one. In terms of personal survival, fighting back may be futile. It takes guts, skill and above all luck to survive an attack by more than one armed soldier. The victim will probably be gravely harmed (possibly killed) no matter what he does, but no matter how grim that may sound, if he has a strategy for defence and gives it his all, he'll at least go down fighting.

However, there are often good military reasons why a soldier tries to defend himself in this kind of situation. One is that it may delay an attack on comrades, or at least the commotion may give them warning of what is coming. Another is that the fight itself may generate intelligence. For example, by disrupting infiltrators' plans through fighting back, the soldier may be putting them into a position where they make mistakes and leave evidence of who they are and what they are up to.

Index

**PAGE NUMBERS IN ITALICS
REFER TO PICTURES**

A

aikido 37-8
Applegate, Col. Rex 11
arm grips, escape *122*
armlocks *102-3*, 106-7
assassinations 111

B

balance 48-9
  blocks *96-7*
  knocking off 137-8, *138*
bayonet attacks *164*
  countering *174-5*, *176-8*
  slashes 177
  thrusts 177, 179
bear hugs, countering 125, *132-3*
biting 75, 119, *119*
blocks
  arms 99, *100*
  balance *96-7*
  and counters *32-3*, 98
  kicks *80*, 100
  lead-hand punches 98
  legs 101
  rear-hand punches 98
  rising *50*
  stance 97-8, *99*, 100-1
  uppercuts 98
Bodhidharma 26, 27
body
  weapons 42, 44, 122
boxing *95*
British Army
  Parachute Regiment *40-41*
  training *30*, 47, *66*

C

China
  kung fu 25-7, 29, 31-2
  martial arts 7-8

chokes
  see also headlocks
  breaking 129-30, *130-31*, 132, 133
  claw squeeze 104-5
  collar *106-7*
  fist *104*
  forearm 106, 107, *109*, *111*
  hair hold *108*
  legs *115*
  reverse naked 109
  scissors *104*
  sentries 109-10, *112-13*
  sliding reverse collar-lock 109
  underarm upward *110*
  upper throat lift 109
cinema, martial arts 16
Close-Quarters Combat [CQC] 21, 61
club attacks
  backhand 183
  defence against *180-81*, *182*
  forehand 182-3
  overhand 182
counter-terrorism 47
cudgel sticks *71*

D

D'Amato, Cus 65, 69
danger
  attitudes to 64
  reaction to 65-6
defences, frontal attacks 122-5, *122-4*
disarming *120-21*
drills
  blind alley 51
  combat alley 51
  pairs 50
  tag-team 50
  two-man combat 50
  wave attack 50
dummies 58-9

E

Egyptian army
  commandos *134-5*

Rangers *22-3*, *50*
special forces 9, *27*, *32-3*
elbow strikes *42*, 112, 114, *153*
  downward 114, *114*, *126*
  reverse 114, 116
  roundhouse *127*
  side 114, *127*
escrima 38
eye attacks *31*, 122

F

Fairburn, William Ewert 24-5
falls 18
  breaking *46*, *54*, 143-4, *144*
  shoulder rolls *144*
fighting distances 18
firearms
  blasts from 151-2
  butt strokes 179, *179*
  defence 158-9
  disarming *20*, *150-51*, *156-7*, *158-9*
  long-barrelled 152, *152*
  to the back *154*, *155*, 157
  to the chest 157
  to the head *153*, *153*, *155-7*
  and unarmed combat 9, 11, 18
fitness
  aerobic 61
  anaerobic 61
  body blows 101
focus pads 48, *52*, *55*, 57-8
French army *33*, 61
frontal attacks, defences 122-5, *122-4*
fundamentals, unarmed combat 25

G

gladiators 9
Graeco-Roman wrestling 26
ground defence
  8, 19, *145*, 147, *147*, 149, *149*
  against firearms *158-9*
  against kicks 147, *147*
  prone position 144, 146
  sitting 147, 149

H

hand strikes
see also punches
edge 90-92
finger jab *86-7*
hammer-fist *42*, *127*
heel of **87**
Hand-to-hand Combat Manual,
 US Army **47**
head butts
forward 117-18, *118*
upward 118, *118*
headlocks *19*
frontal 110-12
release from *128-9*, **133**
side 106, **129**

I

India, martial arts 8-9
Israeli Army
Krav Maga **47**, **116**
training **11**

J

Japan
aikido 37-8
ju-jitsu 32-4
karate *28-9*, 34-5, 38-9
Ninja **81**
Samurai **25**, 33-4, *64*
ju-jitsu 32-4
judo **34**

K

karate *28-9*, 34-5, 38-9
kick boxing *14-15*, **38**, *39*, *72-3*
kicks
against knives *162-3*
blocking *83*, **100**
catching *78*, *133*
flying *90*, *91*, **92**
front **59**, *83*, *90*, **94**
ground defence **147**, *147*
high *10*, 94-5
knee *52*, **58**, **59**, **61**
risks **94**
roundhouse **44**, 57-8, *92-3*, **95**

side *43*, *91*, *94*
snap **57**
targets *84-5*, *92*, *94*
thrust *43*
knee strikes
drops 116, **117**
forward **116**
round-house 116-17
upward 116, *117*, *142-3*
knife attacks
backhand slash 166-7
defence 161-4, **166**
forehand slash 167-8
kicking *162-3*
lunge **164**, *165*, **166**
overhead stabs **168**
psychology of *163-4*
throat *160-61*, *169*, *170-71*, *172-3*
upward stabs **168**, **172**
knives, military **173**
Krav Maga **47**, **116**
kung fu
bok hok pai **31**
choy lee fut 31-2
hsing-i **29**
hung gar **31**
origins **25**, **26**
pa-kua **29**
praying mantis **29**, **31**
tai chi chuan **27**, **29**
wing chun **27**

L

Lee, Bruce **16**, **38**
leg
blocks **101**
chokes *115*
holds *30*
sweeps *36*
target points 80-81
lip tears **122**, *124*

M

makiwara posts *42*, **51**
martial arts
aikido 37-8
China 7-8

escrima **38**
external [hard] 25-6
India 8-9
internal [soft] **26**
ju-jitsu 32-4
karate *28-9*, 34-5, 38-9
Krav Maga **47**, **116**
kung fu 25-7, **29**, 31-2
ninjitsu **81**
taekwando **37**, **92**
mental training
attitude **67**
neutrality **13**, **15**
pain control **67**
relaxation **49**, **67**
ruthlessness **15**, **66**
self-control 64-6
visualisation 67-9, **71**
milling *40-41*
Monaco, Carabiniers *44*
multiple attacks
circle **189**
line 188-9
tactics 185-6
three attackers *187-9*, **188**
two attackers 186-8

N

neck breaks
sentries 109-10
sitting **107**, **109**
neck holds *125*
Ninja **81**
ninjitsu **81**

O, P

pain control **67**
peace-keeping operations **24**, 45-7
Philippines, escrima **38**
posture, stable **18**
pressure points **83**
punchbags *43*, **59**
punches
see also hand strikes
counters to 97-8
follow-up *84-5*, **87**, **88**
jaw 87-8

left hook **88**
left uppercut **88**, *89*, **90**
reverse *45*
right cross **90**

Q, R
Rangers, training *16*
reactions, instinctive **19-20**
relaxation **49**, **67**
restraint techniques **46-7**
Russian army
  Airborne *45*
  Alpha Force *24*
  Close-Quarters Combat **21**
  Spetsnaz
    6-7, *10*, *13*, **47**, **61**, *80*, *84-5*, *184-5*
Russian Martial Art [RMA] **21**

S
safety warnings **71**, **104**
Samozashchitya Bez Oruzhiya
  [Sambo] **21**
Samurai *25*, **33-4**, *64*
sentries **109-10**, *112-13*, **140**
Shaolin temple **26**, **27**, **32**
South Korean army
  taekwando **37**, **92**
  tukong moosul **47**
Spanish army, GEO **61**
speed ball **61**
Spetsnaz
  6-7, *10*, *13*, **47**, **61**, *80*, *84-5*, *184-5*
  karate *6-7*
  Spetsrota *10*
spitting **119**
stance, warrior **48-9**, **97-8**
strangles *see* chokes; headlocks
stress

physiology **18**
psychology **18**
stretching **50**, *55-60*
survival training **51**, **52-3**
Swiss Army, Grenadier School
  8, *36*, *142-3*
Sykes, Maj. William **24**

T
taekwondo **37**, **92**
target points
  abdomen **82-3**
  arms **80**, *80*
  crotch **81-2**
  ears **79**
  eyes **79**
  jaw **75**, **79**
  legs **80-81**
  neck **79-80**
  nose **79**
  selecting **12**, **13**, **73-5**, **82**, *82*
  skull **75**
  spine **82**
Thai boxing **14-15**, **38**, *39*, *72-3*
Thai Rangers *146*, *169*
throws
  countering **140**
  follow-up *9*, **137**
  from behind **76-7**
  front *138*
  hip *35*, *54*, *74-5*, *134-5*, **140**
  leg sweep *139*, *141*
  sentries **140**
  shoulder *33*, *136-7*, *136-7*
  use of **135-6**
  wrist **140**
training
  quick-fix **53**, **55**

realism **15-16**, **53**
repetition **20**
specific **44-5**, *51-3*
stage one **50-51**
warm-ups **50**, *55-60*

U
uniforms, fighting in **53**, **61**
US Army
  Hand-to-hand Combat Manual **47**
  Rangers *16*
  training **11**, *16*, *35*, **47**
US Marines *54*, *68*, *95*
U.S.A., martial arts **38-9**
U.S.S.R. *see* Russian army

V
visualisation
  concrete **71**
  importance **67-9**
  simple **69**, **71**

W
warm-ups **50**, *55-60*
weapons
  body **42**, **44**, **122**
  firearms **9**, **11**, **18**, **45**, **151-9**, **179**
  knives **161-73**
  opportune **16**, **172**
  repellants **65**
World War II **25**
wristlocks *125-6*
  release from **128-9**, *130*
  reverse **128**

X, Y, Z
yoga **67**

PICTURE CREDITS

Leo Docherty: 65, 68, 120-121, 125. **Mary Evans Picture Library:** 25, 26, 64, 67. **Military Picture Library:** 6-7, 10, 13, 80, 84-85, 184-185. **Frank Spooner Pictures:** 24, 28-29, 33 (b), 44, 96-97, 134-135, 146, 155, 169. **Sporting Pictures (UK) Ltd:** 12, 14-15, 39, 72-73. **TRH Pictures:** 9, 16 (US Army), 19 (US Department of Defense), 22-23 (US Department of Defense / USAF), 27, 30 (Ministry of Defence), 32-33, 34 (US Department of Defense), 35, 40-41, 45, 47 (US Department of Defense), 50 (US Department of Defense / USAF), 54 (US Department of Defense / US Marine Core), 62-63, 66, 70, 78, 83, 95 (US Department of Defense), 164, 179, 180-181. **P. Valpolini:** 8, 17, 36, 142-143. **VS Books/Carl Schulze:** 20, 31, 102-103, 108, 133, 139, 150-151, 160-161, 174-175, 182.